PATTERNS *for*
SPECIAL OCCASIONS

PATTERNS

for

SPECIAL

OCCASIONS

Ann Ladbury

B. T. Batsford Ltd, London

ISBN 0 7134 5617 5 (cased)

Typeset by Keyspools Ltd
and printed in Great Britain by
Courier International, Tiptree, Essex
for the publishers
B. T. Batsford Ltd
4 Fitzhardinge Street
London W1H 0AH

Contents

Acknowledgements

I extend my grateful thanks for their help to Cheryl Owen, for cutting the patterns, and to Hazel Merson and Janet Bell for making up the outfits for photography. Janet Bell also worked the decoration on the black velvet skirt, and designed and executed the cutwork border on the black and red linen outfit.

My thanks to Wendy Crease for organizing the photography sessions and to the Marlborough Hotel, Ipswich, for allowing us to use their rooms for photography.

I am indebted to Selectus Limited, the manufacturers of Panda Ribbons and Velcro, for all the photographs in the book including those on the front and back covers.

The Vilene chart on page 18 is reproduced by kind permission of Freudenberg Non-wovens Vilene Retail.

The fabrics for the outfits were generously provided by a number of small shops in various parts of the country. In all cases I was invited to select whatever I liked, regardless of cost or quantity and I am very grateful to all the people listed at the end of the book.

If you live near one of these shops you are lucky. Naturally it is unlikely that they will still have the fabric shown in the photograph, but you will find a selection including, I am sure, something to suit your needs.

I have also included several mail-order companies which offer a good selection of fabrics and colours. I have found their services excellent and my thanks go to them as well.

Harlequin generously made up the matching bags, earrings, bows, etc., for which my grateful thanks.

Introduction

One dark and freezing night, changing trains at Peterborough, I listened to two university students talking about breaking the news to their parents that they needed evening dresses. An hour later we were still waiting for the train but they had decided to make their dresses and I had had the idea for this book.

Clothes for special occasions are not worn often, so I have tried to suggest quick methods of construction which eliminate some of the tedious detail that is usually included on clothes that get a lot of hard wear. At the same time, you want them to look good and not fall apart, so when I suggest it is worth doing something well I really mean it.

There are plenty of sewing aids available which lend themselves particularly well to these clothes, and I have suggested their use as often as possible.

In addition to a wide range of versatile patterns, I have included a selection of decorative features which are easy to do and are stunningly effective ways to individualize your outfits.

1 How to Use this Book

The information in this book is arranged so that you can extract what you need for each project.

If you want to make one of the outfits shown in the photographs, refer to the accompanying instructions. These will tell you which pattern to use, and pages 11–12 explain how to transfer the various patterns to your chosen fabric. The instructions for each outfit give full step-by-step details for making up the garment; extra information is given in the section starting on page 123.

If you prefer to design your own outfit, combining various features in your own way, you will find the fabric quantities and sewing instructions for variations to the basic patterns in the section starting on page 33.

For fabric guidance, there is a chart on pages 19–24 explaining the properties of different fabrics and how to treat them. There are other sections on seam and hem techniques which are helpful if you are sewing a fabric for the first time.

A separate section on decorative techniques will give you ideas for making a special outfit quite unique.

Measurements

All measurements are shown in millimetres, centimetres and metres, with inches and yards following. The conversions are rarely exact and, where such things as shape and fabric thickness come in, it would not be sensible or necessary to be exact. You will, however, find it best to follow either metric or imperial measurements throughout rather than to mix the two scales.

Abbreviations

SG	straight grain of fabric	in	inches
CF	centre front	m	metres
CB	centre back	yd	yards
mm	millimetres	RS	right side of fabric
cm	centimetres	WS	wrong side of fabric

Fabric Quantities

Amounts of fabric are quoted for individual items in 115 cm (45 in) wide fabric, the most common width available. The quantities for the outfits in the photographs are given for the specific fabric used at the start of the making instructions.

When planning your own versions and combinations, you can add together the amounts required for various features. You may be able to economize if you prepare the pattern and lay it out on an odd length of fabric to check it before buying your chosen fabric.

Quantities are not quoted for belts and other features that vary in size but require relatively little fabric. Decorative features such as rosettes and puffs can be made from scraps, but you may need to buy extra for belts. Make a calculation by making the pattern and measuring it.

Nap

All the fabric quantities quoted are for fabrics with a one-way design or print, weave or nap. You may be able to economize by dovetailing pattern pieces. To be sure of the amount required, prepare the pattern and lay it out at home before buying the fabric.

This also applies if you wish to use a width of fabric that is not quoted.

Seam Allowances

The standard amount of 1.5 cm ($\frac{5}{8}$ in) is included on the majority of seams on the patterns. There are some exceptions and these are clearly indicated with the pattern details.

Hem allowances vary. On straight hems and where weight is advisable, 3 cm ($1\frac{1}{4}$ in) has been allowed. On shaped hems, the allowance is for a narrow hem only, 1 cm ($\frac{3}{8}$ in) or 6 mm ($\frac{1}{4}$ in).

No hem allowance has been left on the edges of frills where it is likely that the raw edge would be zigzagged, overlocked, trimmed with pinking shears or, in the case of net or lace, left raw.

All hem allowances are clearly stated with the pattern details. Read them before you start and make adjustments when cutting out if necessary.

Sizes and Body measurements

All the patterns have been cut to the following scale of basic measurements:

Size	12	14	16	18	20
Bust	88 cm ($34\frac{3}{4}$ in)	92 cm ($36\frac{1}{4}$ in)	96 cm ($37\frac{3}{4}$ in)	100 cm ($39\frac{1}{4}$ in)	104 cm (41 in)
Waist	70 cm ($27\frac{1}{2}$ in)	73 cm ($28\frac{3}{4}$ in)	78.5 cm ($30\frac{3}{4}$ in)	82 cm ($32\frac{1}{4}$ in)	87 cm ($34\frac{1}{4}$ in)
Hips	94 cm (37 in)	98 cm ($38\frac{1}{2}$ in)	102 cm (40 in)	106 cm ($41\frac{3}{4}$ in)	110 cm ($43\frac{1}{4}$ in)

Selecting the size

You probably already know where your figure deviates from

average, and you should make your usual adjustments to the pattern pieces after you have prepared them for use. If you fall between two sizes, use the larger one and fit the garment before stitching. If only one or two of your basic measurements correspond with the three given for your size, choose the correct bust size and adjust at waist and hips when cutting out, or use a different size pattern for that part of the garment.

Checking the pattern

Bodice length

Surprisingly, it is just as important to check the length of a strapless pattern as it is a complete bodice. You will know if you are long-waisted or long-backed, so add extra to the pattern pieces at the waist. If you are short-waisted, the bodice can be adjusted at the fitting. Incidentally, if you are short-waisted you may be wise to add straps as you may find it difficult to keep a strapless bodice up.

Lengthen the camisole and cap sleeve patterns, if necessary, by adding extra to the hem; this is especially important if you plan to wear them tucked into a skirt.

Dress and jacket length

Measure the pattern from back neck to hem and compare with your own measurement. If you need it longer and you have long legs, add extra at the hem. If, on the other hand, you are long in the body, cut the pattern pieces across just above waist level and insert extra paper. If the pattern is slightly too long, adjust it at the hem when completing the garment. If it is much too long, you can maintain the balance of the shape and also economize on fabric if you shorten it. To do this, make a horizontal fold across the pattern pieces below waist level.

Sleeve length

Check the long-sleeve patterns by comparing the length of the underarm seam with that on the sleeve of a garment already in your wardrobe. Lengthen or shorten the pattern below the elbow by cutting and inserting extra paper, or by folding out a horizontal pleat.

Skirt length

For long skirts, hold a tape measure so that it hangs from your waist and read off the required measurement. Lengthen or shorten skirt patterns at the hemline. With some of the diagram patterns and those giving measurements only, this adjustment can be made when you draw the pattern.

Trousers

Compare the length of the inside leg seam of the pattern with that of a pair of trousers in your wardrobe. Lengthen or shorten at the hemline. Compare the side seam length in the same way. Lengthen or shorten the pattern pieces mid-way between waist and crutch level by inserting extra paper, or by folding out a horizontal pleat. In addition to this, trousers should always be fitted before stitching so that other adjustments can be made, notably to the hang by lifting or dropping the front or back waist, or by reshaping the crotch seam.

With all the above pattern adjustments, remember the following:
(a) Omit all hem and seam allowances when measuring.
(b) Adjust the length of the corresponding pattern pieces so that the seams still match. (The exception is the length of frills, which can remain the same.)

Larger and smaller sizes

Sizes covered in the book are 12, 14, 16, 18 and 20. Apologies if you are smaller or larger, but all the shapes are simple and it would not be difficult to increase or reduce the pattern, as follows.

Add or subtract 13 mm ($\frac{1}{2}$ in) on each edge of the side seams for each size. For example, for size 22 cut out with an extra 13 mm ($\frac{1}{2}$ in) added to the side seam on back and front. Curve to meet the armhole and add the same amount to the sleeve seams. For size 24, it would be better to cut the pattern from mid-shoulder to mid-hem, spread the pieces and insert 2.5 cm (1 in) between the cut edges.

For a smaller pattern, subtract these amounts. If you are nervous of making alterations, an alternative method is to place these patterns on top of some that you have already in the correct size and use them as your guide.

The Patterns

The main pattern pieces are printed on the pattern sheet at the back of the book. Others are shown as diagram patterns to be scaled up to full size. The simplest patterns, for frills, straps and gathered skirts, can be cut following the measurements given. With most of these, you could mark the size directly on the fabric without making a paper pattern, provided you are sure of the position of the remaining pieces of pattern and that you have sufficient fabric.

The Full-size Patterns

Select the pieces required and cut out, following the line shown for your size. Check that you have the correct number of pieces. Press with a warm iron ready for use.

If you wish to keep the pattern sheet intact, trace the shapes required onto tracing paper, pattern drafting paper or, for a durable pattern, soft sew-in Vilene.

Copy all the information onto your pattern, including size, straight grain lines and balance marks (notches). After use, store in a polythene bag, insert a scrap of the fabric you used and put in a note of any special sewing or fitting points.

Drawing the Diagram Patterns

Each square represents 2.5 cm (1 in)

This takes a little time but is not difficult. Locate the garment you wish to make and your size. Transfer the shapes onto squared pattern paper. Begin at one corner of the pattern, ruling an angle or straight line to start with. Count the number of squares up and across at each major point and rule all the straight lines. Fill in the curves: a dotted line is easier to draw than a solid line.

Alternatively, use sheets of plain pattern drafting paper or sew-in Vilene. Spread this over a cutting board; the printed squares on the board will be clearly visible.

Transfer all the instructions to the pattern pieces, including size, straight grain lines and balance marks (notches). Cut out the pattern and check corresponding seam edges for accuracy. After use, store in a polythene bag with a scrap of the fabric used and any relevant notes.

Making Patterns from Measurements

Follow the measurements and instructions given. In some cases the measurements are the same for all sizes.

Mark out the shape required either with a pencil and ruler on pattern paper, or directly onto WS of your fabric using tailor's chalk or a fabric pen and a ruler.

Note: The pen marks disappear in 6–24 hours but to be safe, especially on expensive silks, test on a scrap of fabric and wait for the marks to fade before using on the actual garment. If, despite this, you are left with a mark, it can be washed out. Do not iron over pen marks or they may become fixed.

The Possibilities

Patterns and instructions have been given for a variety of garments, for decorations to and for accessories. The real choice is even wider, for the patterns are versatile and can be used for quite different garments. In addition, the pattern pieces can be combined in a variety of ways. If you then consider the fabrics you can use and the fact that it is your choice of fabric that creates your individual outfit, you can see that there is something in the book for every possible special occasion.

2 The Basics

Sewing Equipment

This is not a comprehensive list of equipment because you probably already have the basics. It is more a reminder of some of the tools that are available and make sewing so much easier. If you are a beginner, you will still find them a help but you will also need scissors, pins, needles, a tape measure and basting thread.

Fading marking pen
The marks fade within 24 hours but on fine or delicate fabrics it may be wise to test first. It is very useful for marking darts, zip points, gathered areas, etc.

Iron cleaner
Rub this stick on your iron to remove scorch marks and adhesive from iron-on products. It is a wise precaution to clean your iron before pressing pale or delicate fabrics.

Tape maker
This is used for making folded bias strips from fabric. It is well worth buying as bias binding is widely used in the patterns in this book. Tape makers are available in two sizes, the smaller one taking a strip 2.5 cm (1 in) wide. Press the strip as it emerges and the binding is ready for use.

Cutting board
This large, lightweight board unfolds to cover a table or even a bed to provide a cutting-out surface. It has useful markings and one type has a basic pattern printed on one side.

Embroidery hoop
There may be a small hoop in your sewing machine accessory box for working machine embroidery. A larger hoop for hand embroidery is useful for working beading and quilting, and also when making fabric puffs.

Basting tape

A narrow tape with peel-off backing, this is either single- or double-sided. It is very useful on zips in place of basting, and has many other uses.

Rouleau needle

This is invaluable for making fine tubing. After stitching the fabric, insert the rouleau needle and sew the eye to the end of the tube. Ease all the fabric onto the needle, pull it out and the tube will turn RS out. It is also useful for turning belts and threading elastic.

Adjustable marker

A short metal rule with a movable marker, this is useful for repeated measuring, e.g. hem depth, parallel stitching, width of tucks, length of buttonholes.

Tweezer bodkin

This pointed plastic tool has tweezers set into the opposite end. Use the point for easing out corners and removing basting; use the tweezers for removing stubborn thread ends.

Beading needle

A very long, very fine needle for sewing on beads, this will pass through even the smallest hole and its length means that you can slip several beads on at a time. It penetrates several layers easily, e.g. quilting, padded appliqué.

Spiked tracing wheel

Use this for copying patterns. Place a sheet of tracing paper or pattern paper over the pattern to be copied and use the tracing wheel to mark the outline. To make several copies, put the sheets of paper beneath the pattern and run the wheel round the pattern, pressing hard onto the paper beneath. It can also be used for marking one or two layers of compressed or shiny fabric, such as taffeta or satin.

Smooth tracing wheel

This is used for transferring pattern markings to fabric. Use it with dressmaker's carbon paper, cut into strips and folded with the colour outside. With the pattern still pinned to the fabric, slide the carbon paper between the two layers of fabric then run the wheel over the markings of the pattern and the lines will appear on WS of each piece of fabric. Do not use carbon paper on white or pale-coloured fabric as it may show through to RS.

In case of difficulty in obtaining any of these products, write to Harlequin whose address is on page 126.

Haberdashery

The following can be used to advantage on the outfits in this book. They help you achieve good results, they are quick to use and they are reliable.

Velcro
This can be used in a variety of places, including waist fastenings and on the flap of a bag. It is available in strip form, in a variety of colours. It helps to trim $2\,\text{mm}$ ($\frac{1}{16}\,\text{in}$) off the hook or firm side so that it is completely covered when the loop or soft side is pressed against it.

Velcro Spot-Ons
These small discs have adhesive on the back, which makes them adhere to the fabric while you sew round them. They are sold in pre-packs, in several colours.

Hooks on tape
Available in black and white, these are a neat, quick way of fastening a long opening instead of using a zip.

Curved petersham
For many people, waistbands and belts are more comfortable if they are shaped. Curved petersham can be used to stiffen both; it can also be stitched directly to the waist of a skirt, dispensing with a waistband.

Fold-a-Band
This is an interfacing strip with a line of central perforations. It is a quick and accurate way of making straps, bands, waistbands and cuffs. Lightweight Fold-a-Band is a net width, with a seam allowance of fabric to be added when cutting out. Heavy Fold-a-Band, for waistbands, has a seam allowance included, marked by perforations, and comes in various widths. Both are available in packs and by the metre. With both, you simply cut the length required, press it to WS of the fabric and cut out round the outside edge.

Wundaweb
This narrow web is inserted under a hem fold. When pressed, the Wundaweb melts and bonds the hem in place. It is not suitable for fine fabrics but is very good for trouser and straight skirt hems in medium-weight and firm fabrics. See page 32 for instructions. If in doubt, test first.

Stitch 'n' Tear
This stiff, papery sheet is used as a base for embroidery and other decorative sewing. It also helps to prevent puckered seams in fine fabrics. Tear away the surplus afterwards, although if the firmness is still useful, e.g. in a bag, it can be left in place.

Bondaweb

This is similar to Wundaweb but with a paper backing which enables it to be pressed into position and, when cool, the fabric can be handled before being pressed against another piece of fabric. It is useful for preventing fraying in small areas, also for joining layers of fabric, e.g. in appliqué.

Fray Check

A colourless liquid in a small bottle, this is applied to the edges of fraying fabric. It is particularly useful if the fabric is to be handled a lot, e.g. embroidery or other decorative work.

Mesh elastic

Mesh elastic is light and transparent, and available in black and white in several widths. It can be applied direct to WS fabric, using zigzag stitch and stretching the elastic as you stitch. Mesh elastic has a less firm grip than conventional elastic.

Rigilene

Polyester boning for bodices, bags, etc. Cut to length and insert in casings made with bias strips or attach directly to WS fabric or lining by machining along each edge.

Threads

For general sewing, most people use whatever thread can be bought locally. But if you are visiting a department store or specialist fabric shop to buy the fabric for your outfit, that is your chance to buy the threads required and also to stock up on other colours you might be short of.

As well as deciding which outfit to make, think about any decorative techniques or stitching you might want to use and buy the thread for those too.

Thread for the outfit

For most outfits, buy two 100-metre reels; for a long dress, one with frills, or an outfit of two or more pieces, buy three. If your fabric is black or white, buy one 500-metre reel instead.

Choose a darker rather than a matching or lighter thread. If you decide on contrasting stitching on the outside of the garment, remember that it will show more than a matched thread.

Spun polyester thread, e.g. Drima, is suitable for all fabrics, of any weight or type. It is strong, it beds down well into the fabric when pressed with an iron, it is fine and yet it has 'give', which means the seams will not split. It is suitable for both hand and machine stitching.

Silk thread, although not readily available, can be used on silk fabric but it is comparatively thick.

Thread for basting

Use proper basting or tacking thread, e.g. Atlas. It is soft and fluffy, which means that it will not harm even the finest of fabrics and it will hold well in slippery fabrics.

An alternative for fine fabrics is to use machine embroidery thread. Never use Drima or other sewing thread. It is very wasteful and it is also too strong; it can easily damage the fabric, so you have to spend longer removing it. Basting thread can simply be pulled out.

Thread for machine embroidery

For fine stitching, use Anchor Machine Embroidery Thread No. 50. Use No. 30 for topstitching or heavier embroidery.

Glitter threads, e.g. Effektgarn, are effective for quilting as well as machine embroidery.

Interfacing

Interfacing is required in various parts of the clothes described in this book, not to prolong wear, as would normally be the case, but rather to provide support or shape, or a base firm enough to take decoration.

If you are making an outfit for an occasion but at the same time with the deliberate intention of giving it normal wear afterwards, you would do well to give particular consideration to the type of fabric to be used and to revise the suggestions for interfacing specified in the list on page 18.

For interfacing grades required for fabrics other than those listed, please refer to the chart over the page.

The type and weight of interfacing suggested is a guide only. Some lightweight fabrics may not require interfacing at all. Some areas may need additional reinforcement or a heavier weight of interfacing to produce a particular effect. For example, the strapless bodice could be backed with medium-weight Vilene and the bag and cummerbund will probably require heavy or pelmet-weight Vilene to stiffen them.

Test all fusible or iron-on interfacing on a scrap of fabric. Always use a damp cloth. If a mark or line is visible, change to a sew-in product. If one layer of iron-on interfacing is not enough, add another.

Vilene interfacing	Description	Application	Fabric weight	Suggested fabric
ultrasoft – light 308 – fusible white 309 – fusible charcoal	no grainline, non-stretch, washable and dry cleanable	collars, facings, cuffs, soft features, bows, yokes, full fronts, back yokes	soft to delicate	voile, chiffon, silk, crêpe-de-chine, lawn, georgette, polyester, cotton, poly-cotton, lightweight wools
light – sew-in 310 – white 311 – charcoal	no grainline, washable and dry cleanable	collars, cuffs, facings, yokes	soft, delicate or lightweight	polyester, silk, lawn, cotton, seersucker, panné, velvet
ultrasoft – medium 315 – fusible white	no grainline, non-stretch, washable and dry cleanable	collars, facings, full fronts, back yokes for suits, sleeve edges, soft belts	light to medium	challis, poplin, wool, wool blends, linen, cotton, jacket-weight silks
medium – sew-in 312 – white	no grainline, washable and dry cleanable		light to medium	corduroy, velvet
ultrasoft – medium 315 – fusible white ultrasoft – heavy 316 – fusible white	no grainline, non-stretch, washable and dry cleanable	full fronts, lapels, collars, facings, shoulders, suits and coats, belts, craft applications	medium to heavy	gaberdine, tweeds, suit and coat-weight wools and woollen mixtures
heavy – sew-in 313 – white	no grainline, washable and dry cleanable		medium to heavy	
superstretch 319 – fusible white	has grainline, lengthwise stability and crosswise stretch, washable and dry cleanable	collars, cuffs, facings, soft features, bows, yokes, full fronts, sleeve edges, cut and sew	light to medium	lightweight knits, jersey, polyester, double knits
medium – iron-on 304 – white	no grainline, light crisp handle, washable only	collars, cuffs, facings and other small-area applications	light to medium	cotton and cotton-blend fabrics
firm – iron-on 305 – white	no grainline, firm crisp handle, washable only	collars, cuffs, facings and other small-area applications	medium to heavy	cotton and cotton-blend fabrics

Fabrics and their properties

Iron settings

These are shown as:

    o – Cool

   oo – Warm

ooo – Hot

Use a steam iron if possible.

Fabric	Seams	Needle	Stitch	Iron	Interface
Acetate poult Cheap, slightly ribbed, crisp fabric used for lining but quite suitable for full-style evening dresses.	Open or overlocked	80–11	Medium	o	Ultrasoft Light
Acetate satin Inexpensive, crisp, medium weight. Creases and frays. Good under transparent fabrics and for piping and binding.	Open	80–11	Medium	o	Ultrasoft Light or light sew-in Vilene
All-over lace Inexpensive; often regular floral design all over. Easy to sew.	Hairline, narrow or overlapped Avoid deep hems	70–9	Medium	o	Net
Antung silk Cheap, crisp. Use for lining and under transparent fabrics.	Open	80–11	Medium	oo	Ultrasoft Light
Brocade Crisp, can be heavy, with ornate designs in matching, contrast, silver or gold yarns. Frays badly.	Open, control fraying with net binding or overlock Deep hems, possibly Wundaweb	80–11	Medium	o	Ultrasoft Medium or net
Broderie anglaise Crisp, ornate cotton or cotton with polyester. Use for overdress, frills, flounces.	French or narrow Avoid deep hems	80–11	Medium	ooo	Iron-on Vilene, cut away behind eyelets
Chantilly lace Expensive, but soft and beautiful. May have scalloped edge. Needs lining. Sleeves, etc. can be stiffened with net.	Overlap Avoid deep hems	80–11	Medium	o on towel	Net or organdie
Charmeuse Slightly lustrous satin-weave fabric made from any of the soft yarns, including cotton. Creases and frays. Inexpensive.	Open or overlocked	70–9	Medium	o	Ultrasoft Light or light sew-in Vilene

Fabric	Seams	Needle	Stitch	Iron	Interface
Chiffon Soft, transparent. Frays easily. Polyester chiffon is thicker and easier to sew than silk. Stitch with paper or Stitch 'n' Tear beneath if seams wrinkle.	Hairline or narrow Avoid deep hems	70–9	Small	○	
Crêpe-back satin Floppy and soft, with a rich appearance. Either side can be RS, both sides can be featured in one outfit. Even if made from silk yarn, it creases very little.	Open or overlocked	70–9	Medium	○○	Light sew-in Vilene
Crêpe de chine Light, soft, matt fabric that drapes well. Expensive in silk yarn but luxurious.	French or narrow	90–9	Small	○	Light sew-in Vilene
Embossed velvet Usually a mixture such as viscose/cotton/modal to create the variation in design. Luxurious effect. Expensive but worth it.	Open or overlocked	80–11	Large	○ on wrong side	Light sew-in Vilene
Embroidered flouncing Light, plain cotton, viscose, or polyester cotton, with embroidered scallops on one or both edges.	Open or French	80–11	Medium	○	Ultrasoft Light
Embroidered knit Fine polyester knit fabric with coloured or metal decoration which may be stitched or stuck in place. Does not fray or crease.	Narrow or overlocked	70–9 Ballpoint	Medium	○ on wrong side only	Super-stretch iron-on
Embroidered organza Soft fabric for overdresses. Expensive; may have scalloped edge.	Hairline, narrow or overlocked	80–11	Medium	○	
Embroidered polyester taffeta Elaborate patterns, often including diamanté. Expensive.	Open	80–11	Medium	○	Light or medium sew-in Vilene
Faconné Soft silk, polyester or viscose with woven pattern.	French or narrow	70–9	Small	○	Light sew-in Vilene
Faille taffeta Firm ribbed taffeta with a rich appearance.	Open or overlocked	70–9	Medium	○○	Ultrasoft Light or medium

Fabric	Seams	Needle	Stitch	Iron	Interface
Flecked metallic jersey Usually a close white jersey backing sprayed with flexible metallic finish and with contrast spots, stripes, etc. stuck on. Stunning effects and expensive, but easy to sew.	Open or overlocked	80–11	Large	—	Medium sew-in Vilene if required
Flock spot net Interesting attractive net for panels, flounces and overdresses.	Hairline	70–9	Small	○	Plain net
Fringed tissue Crisp, synthetic taffeta-weave fabric with fringing in checks or stripes providing interesting texture. Cut pattern pieces with fringe lying downwards.	Open or overlocked	70–9	Medium	○	Ultrasoft Light
Georgette Soft, springy, matt fabric, often printed. Frays. Use for full styles. Needs lining.	Hairline, French or narrow	70–9	Small	○	—
Gold and silver tissue Fine soft gauze made of silk or polyester with metal. Frays and snags easily.	Hairline	70–9	Small	○	Light sew-in Vilene
Indian silk Crisp, slightly wrinkled fabric in plain colours.	Open or overlocked	80–11	Medium	○	Light sew-in Vilene
Metallic knit Soft and floppy. Stunningly effective, may be smooth, lacy or nobbly. Does not crease or fray.	Narrow or overlocked	70–9 Ballpoint	Medium	○	
Metallic lace Effective instant luxury at reasonable cost. Easy to handle.	Hairline or overlapped	80–11	Medium	○	Net
Moiré Crisp, often thick fabric with ribbed appearance and watermark pattern on RS.	Open	80–11	Large	○	Ultrasoft Light or medium
Net Stiff and rough. Use for overdresses, frills and petticoats, facings, etc. Plain net is cheap, embroidered net is more expensive.	Narrow	70–9	Large	○	—
Ninghai silk Dull-surfaced heavy fabric. Cheap.	Open	80–11	Large	○○	Light sew-in Vilene

Fabric	Seams	Needle	Stitch	Iron	Interface
Organdie Stiff, transparent cotton. Creases. Use for overdresses, sleeves, bows, etc.	Narrow or French	70–9	Small	○○○	—
Organza Stiff, transparent silk; expensive. Use for overdresses, sleeves, bows, etc.	Hairline	80–11	Large	○○	—
Panné velvet Soft, shiny, flat-pile fabric. Expensive but wide. Printed panné is stunning. Needs lining.	Open or overlocked	80–11 Ballpoint	Large	○ on wrong side	
Polyester Crêpe Lovely, soft, matt fabric; cheap. May fray.	Narrow or overlocked Facings may show	70–9	Medium	○	Light sew-in Vilene
Polyester Crêpe de chine Inexpensive soft, fine fabric. Frays; needs lining. Can also be used for lining or underdresses.	French or narrow	80–11	Medium	○	Ultrasoft Light or light sew-in Vilene
Polyester faille Thick, soft fabric in a wide range of excellent colours.	Open or overlocked	70–9	Medium	○○	Ultrasoft Light
Polyester satin Soft and almost crease-free. Varies in weight.	Open or overlocked	80–11	Medium	○	Light sew-in Vilene
Pongée Light, soft fabric in acetate, polyester or sometimes silk. It has little body, but is suitable for lining or as an underdress.	Narrow or overlocked	70–9	Small	○	—
Sequinned fabric Usually narrow width for making tops. Very expensive. Do not line, but raw edges must be covered.	Overlocked	80–11	Large	—	—
Sequinned lace Extravagant-looking fabric without the sewing problems of heavily sequinned fabric. Use for overdresses, flounces, etc.	Hairline or overlocked	80–11	Large	○ on wrong side only	Net
Shantung Slightly rough textured fabric due to uneven yarn. Creases badly if silk. Polyester shantung is a good imitation.	Open or overlocked	70–9	Medium	○○	Ultrasoft Light

Fabric	Seams	Needle	Stitch	Iron	Interface
Shot taffeta Lightweight fabric woven in two colours, giving interesting effects.	Open or overlocked	70–9	Medium	○○	Ultrasoft Light
Silk habutai Cheap and soft, but too thin for outer wear. Use for lining.	French or overlocked	70–9	Small	○	—
Silk jacquard Soft crêpe with satin design; expensive. Does not crease, frays easily.	Open or overlocked	70–9	Small	○	Ultrasoft Light
Silky knit Occasionally silk but more usually polyester. Soft and floppy, drapes well. Does not crease. Cut all pattern pieces in one direction to avoid shading. Avoid hand sewing.	Narrow or overlocked	70–9 Ballpoint	Medium	○○	Super-stretch
Slipper satin Closely woven satin with expensive look due to its comparative lack of shine. Frays; seams may wrinkle.	Open or overlocked	80–11	Medium	○○	Light sew-in Vilene
Spun silk Inexpensive silk with dull surface. Creases and frays. Needs lining to provide body.	Open or overlocked	80–11	Medium	○○○	Ultrasoft Light or light sew-in Vilene
Synthetic jersey Soft knitted fabric, usually lustrous. Does not fray. Cut all pieces in one direction. May be the base for a pile fabric. See also *Silky knit*.	Narrow or overlocked	70–9 Ballpoint	Medium	○	Super-stretch
Taffeta Paper taffeta made from silk is thin and crisp and creases easily. Fabric made from polyester yarns is inexpensive and crease-free. Often has embossed pattern or watermark.	Open or overlocked	70–9	Medium	○	Light sew-in or ultrasoft Light
Thai silk Made from uneven yarn, usually with heavier yarns crosswise causing it to wrinkle. Needs lining. Most successful in small areas as it does not hang well. Frays.	Open or overlocked	80–11	Medium	○○○	Ultrasoft Medium
Tulle Soft and fine with net construction. May be silk or polyester. Use for bows and flounces.	Hairline	80–11	Small	○	—

Fabric	Seams	Needle	Stitch	Iron	Interface
Tussah Heavy, plain silk with uneven texture. Frays. Lightest-weight fabrics can be used for dresses.	Open or overlocked	90–12	Large	○○○	Ultrasoft Medium
Velveteen Usually cotton fibre with short, even pile. May be plain or printed. Easier to sew than true velvet. Cut all pattern pieces in one direction. May have embossed pattern or watermark.	Open or overlocked	80–11	Large	○○ on wrong side only with spare piece of fabric under	Light sew-in or ultrasoft Light
Viscose Panné Soft, shiny, flat-pile fabric. Expensive but wide. Printed panné is stunning. Needs lining.	Open or overlocked	80–11 Ballpoint	Large	○ on wrong side	Ultrasoft Light or light sew-in Vilene
Voile May be cotton, which creases, or polyester, which does not. Easy to sew. Needs lining.	French, narrow or hairline	70–9	Small	○○	Organdie
Wild silk Heavy, plain silk with uneven texture. Frays. Lightweight fabrics can be used for dresses.	Open or overlocked	90–12	Large	○○○	Ultrasoft Medium
Wool georgette Fine, springy fabric that frays and needs lining. May be plain or printed.	Open or overlocked	90–11	Medium	○○	Light sew-in Vilene

Seams

Utility seams

One or more of the following will be suitable for the main seams. Selection should depend on the thickness of the fabric; whether it frays; how firmly it can be pressed; and whether, as in the case of plain, shiny fabrics, the seam allowances are liable to make a ridge. If your experience is limited or if you are using a fabric that is unfamiliar, make a small trial seam first.

Remember that thread must be a perfect colour match if the fabric is transparent, semi-transparent or a pale colour.

Time, and possibly fabric, can be saved by cutting the fabric initially with narrow seam allowances if any of the first four seams are to be used.

Hairline seam

Use for fine, transparent and semi-transparent fabrics. Hold the pieces of fabric RS together. Pin at right angles or baste 2 cm ($\frac{3}{4}$ in) from the edge. Trim just over 1 cm ($\frac{3}{8}$ in) off the raw edges. Using a small, close zigzag stitch, and with paper or Stitch 'n' Tear beneath synthetic or slippery fabrics, stitch and neatly enclose the raw edges. Remove the pins as you meet them; remove the basting on completion. Press the stitching flat, press the seam flat to one side, then press again on RS.

For a stronger seam, if the fabric frays badly, sew a line of small straight stitching 1.5 cm ($\frac{5}{8}$ in) inside the raw edges and remove the pins before trimming. Zigzag as before beside the stitching.

Overlapped seam

Use for lace and fine embroidered net, or transparent fabrics where the design must be matched. With the fabric RS up, overlap one piece onto the other, taking 1.5 cm ($\frac{5}{8}$ in) seam on *both* edges. Baste; pin if it is only a short seam. Use a very small, close zigzag stitch, place paper or Stitch 'n' Tear beneath the fabric and stitch, following the outline of the design as closely as possible. The more wavy the stitching, the less the seam will show. Remove the basting. Trim off the surplus fabric close to the stitching on both sides. Place the seam on a towel and press to keep the embroidery, etc. raised.

Use the same method to rejoin a scalloped edge at the hem edges.

Narrow seam

Use for soft, lightweight opaque fabrics. Hold the pieces of fabric RS together, and pin or baste 2 cm ($\frac{3}{4}$ in) from the edge. Trim 1 cm ($\frac{3}{8}$ in) from the edge. Place slippery fabrics on paper or Stitch 'n' Tear; sew the seam with a wide zigzag stitch, or one that makes alternate straight stitches. Remove the pins as they occur, then remove the basting on completion. Press the stitching flat, and press the seam flat to one side. Press again on RS, protecting shiny fabrics and crêpe with a dry pressing cloth.

For a stronger seam or in order to use a smaller zigzag, sew a line of small straight stitching 1.5 cm ($\frac{5}{8}$ in) inside the raw edges before trimming. Remove the pins, trim and zigzag as before beside the straight stitching.

Overlocked seam

Use for knits and for lightweight and firm fabrics that fray. Hold the pieces of fabric RS together, and pin or baste 3 cm ($1\frac{1}{4}$ in) from the edge. Set an overlocker or overlocking attachment to stitch, trim and neaten the seam. Remove the pins as they occur, then remove the basting on completion. Press the stitching flat, press the seam flat to one side, then press again on RS.

For fitted areas such as the strapless bodice, make a stronger seam by working a row of straight stitching 1.5 cm ($\frac{5}{8}$ in) from the edge before overlocking.

25

French seam
Use for lightweight fabrics that fray. Hold the pieces of fabric WS together, and pin or baste along the seamline. Use a small straight stitch and sew 1 cm ($\frac{3}{8}$ in) from the edge. Remove the pins as they occur; remove the basting on completion. Press the stitching flat. Trim the raw edges to within 3 mm ($\frac{1}{8}$ in) of the stitching. Open out the layers of fabric, press the seam flat to one side and press again on RS. Fold the seam so that the pieces of fabric are RS together. Make sure the seam is exactly on the edge by rolling it between your fingers. Press or baste and press.

Place fine or slippery fabrics on paper, and stitch 5 mm ($\frac{1}{4}$ in) from the edge, using the edge of the machine foot to guide you. Remove the basting. Press the stitching flat, and press the seam flat to one side. On RS, check that no raw edges are visible, trimming them off carefully if necessary, then press again, protecting plain, shiny fabrics with a dry pressing cloth.

Open seam
Use for all except very lightweight fabrics. Hold the pieces of fabric RS together, and pin or baste together. Using a straight stitch, sew 1.5 cm ($\frac{5}{8}$ in) from the edge. Remove the pins as they occur; remove the basting on completion. Press the stitching flat. Open out the fabric and use the tip of the iron to open the seam allowances. Press the seam flat, then press again on RS, protecting plain, shiny fabrics with a dry pressing cloth. On WS, trim the raw edges evenly and neatly. Finish with zigzag or overlock if the fabric frays or if the garment is unlined.

If open seams are wrinkled near the hemline where there is no weight to pull them flat, place narrow strips of Wundaweb, one under each seam allowance, and press with the seam stretched flat and pinned to the pressing surface. Try this first on a scrap of fabric if you are using a shiny fabric such as satin or silk, to ensure that neither watermarks nor press marks appear.

Channel seam
Use where ribbon or narrow elastic is to be inserted. Depending on the feature, one or both edges may have to be gathered. If this is so, begin by inserting gathering threads and marking two, four or eight equal sections. With fabric RS together, stitch along the seamline, first pulling up the gathers if appropriate. Do not trim the seam allowances but stitch again near the raw edges to hold them together. If the fabric frays, add a row of zigzag, although this will reduce the width of the channel. Depending on the design, leave a gap in the stitching for inserting elastic at a later stage.

Make sure the stitching is fastened off securely and neatly where the slot for threading is left. The easiest way to thread elastic or ribbon is to sew or tie it to the end of a rouleau needle (see page 14).

If the fabric is bulky or if the elastic is more than 5 mm ($\frac{1}{4}$ in) in width, allow a wider seam allowance on each edge when cutting out.

Casing seam

An alternative seam to use where boning, elastic or ribbon is to be inserted. Join the pieces of fabric with an open seam, press open and trim both edges to 5 mm ($\frac{1}{4}$ in). For the casing, use bias binding pressed flat, or strips of lining or self fabric 2.5 cm (1 in) wide or 1 cm ($\frac{3}{8}$ in) wider than the item to be inserted. Place the strip RS up evenly over the seam allowances, and baste along the middle. With the garment RS up, stitch each side of the seamline parallel with it and evenly 1 cm ($\frac{3}{8}$ in) from it (or whatever distance is required). If a decorative stitch is used, make sure you do not reduce the width of the channel. Remove all the basting and press. Note that a slot for threading may have to be left either in the seam or on one side of the channel stitching.

Fasten off the stitching threads securely, as for the *Channel seam* above.

Decorative seams

These are seams where the stitching is visible on the outside of the garment or where there are gathers, frills, flounces, etc.

Piped seam

Use at a waistline, the upper edge of a strapless bodice, and the outer edges of a belt, cummerbund or bag. Make lengths of piping from bias strips of matching or contrast fabric 2 cm ($\frac{3}{4}$ in) wide, joining them on SG. Press the strip, stretching it slightly, fold it along the middle, RS out, and press. Firm, filled piping can be made by wrapping a 2.5 cm (1 in) bias strip over thin, pre-shrunk piping cord. Baste the edges of the fabric together close to the cord.

Place the piping on RS of one piece of garment, with 2–3 mm ($\frac{1}{16}$–$\frac{1}{8}$ in) of the fold extending inside the seamline. With filled piping, line up the basting with the seamline. Pin or baste the piping in position. Although you can hold it in place accurately without either, you will finish up with a smoother seam if it has been secured. Stitch 1.5 cm ($\frac{5}{8}$ in) from the garment raw edge to join the piping to the fabric. Use a piping foot on the machine if you are using filled piping. Remove any basting. Press the stitching with the tip of the iron on both sides of the fabric.

Place the second piece of garment RS down over the piping. With the edges level, baste through all layers. Turn the seam over to bring the first row of stitching on top. Sew the seam, following the first row but letting the stitches fall just to the inside. Press the stitching. Open out the fabric and press up to the piping each side. If the seam is at the garment edge, roll the lining to the inside and baste through all layers below the piped edge. If the seam is to be flat, trim and neaten the seam allowances, keeping them together if placed at the waistline.

Welt seam

Use to keep seam allowances flat or where decorative stitching is required. Hold the pieces of fabric RS together and pin or baste. Stitch on the seamline. Press the stitching, then press both seam allowances flat to one side. Trim the edges and zigzag together if the fabric frays or if the garment is unlined. With RS up, stitch again parallel with the seamline, making sure the seam allowances remain flat on the underside. If the fabric is slippery or on the bias, it is wise to baste along the seam first. The type of stitch used and the distance it is placed from the seamline depends on its position and the effect you want.

Suggestions for stitching include one or two rows of matching or contrast straight stitching; twin or triple needle stitching; any zigzag, decorative or embroidery stitch; stitching using gold or silver thread (this may have to be stitched from WS); couching over thread, yarn or narrow ribbon; and hand embroidery.

If the fabric is bulky, trim off the under seam allowance before basting and stitching the seam decoratively.

This seam would be suitable for the strapless bodice where boning is to be used. Make a test seam to determine the position of the final row of stitching in order to allow the boning to be slotted in. Although boning can be inserted in the seams of the main fabric, it is more usual to make the slots in the lining. Leave a gap near the end of the seam or leave the end of the seam accessible. Insert the boning after the garment is complete.

Gathered seam

Use at waistlines, and for frills and skirt tiers. There are two possible methods, the first being easier. The stitching is visible on the outside of the garment but it could be covered with ribbon, embroidery, etc.

For both methods, begin by inserting the gathering threads. Use the largest straight stitch on the machine, even the top stitch, and sew along the seamline. Turn the fabric at right angles, make two stitches, turn again and stitch parallel to the first row. Leave ends of thread 8 cm (3 in) long. When gathering a long piece of fabric such as a skirt or a frill, begin by dividing the edge into two, four, or even eight, inserting separate gathering threads in each section. Always use a polyester or core-spun thread such as Drima or Duet, both of which are strong enough to withstand being pulled.

To make the seam the easiest way, fold under the seam allowance on the second piece of the garment and press. Divide the edge into two, four or eight to correspond with the frill, and mark the points with pins or fabric pen. With the fabric RS up, overlap the folded edge onto the gathered edge, matching the marks. Pin at each point, across the seam. Working on one section at a time, pull up the gathers by taking hold of the *bobbin* threads and easing the fabric along until the edge has been reduced to fit the folded edge. Insert a pin on WS and wind the threads around it to secure. Ease the gathers along until they are evenly spaced. Insert more pins to hold. Baste the section, stitching on RS 3 mm ($\frac{1}{4}$ in) from the fold. Fasten off the basting, remove the pins and move on to the next section. Stitch the seam with the fabric RS up, sewing slowly to make sure the gathers do not bunch. Stitch close to the fold with a straight, zigzag or decorative stitch. Remove the basting. On fine fabrics, remove the gathering threads. Press the stitching with the tip of the iron. On WS, trim both edges to 5 mm ($\frac{1}{4}$ in) and zigzag or overlock together, or insert a second row of stitching from RS.

To make the seam by the second method, divide the edge of the second piece of the garment then place it against the gathered part, RS together. Match and pin together at the marks. Pull up the gathers as above. Baste each section on the seamline. Stitch the seam with straight stitch, with the gathers uppermost. Sew slowly, taking care not to let the gathers bunch. Remove the basting, press the stitching, trim the raw edges and zigzag or overlock together.

Flounce seam
Use where a circular flounce joins the main garment. The finished seam must be as narrow as possible so that it does not restrict the fall of the flounce. Wherever possible, join all the seams and mark the centres of both garment and flounce. With both pieces RS together, match the seams and centres, and pin. Divide each section with more pins. It is quite likely that the flounce edge will seem too big as it is on the bias, but it can be eased in. There may be gathers to insert as a feature.

Hold the seam with the flounce uppermost so that it falls over your hand, and insert more and more pins until the excess has been controlled. Baste the seam with small stitches. Snip both raw edges at intervals of 1 cm ($\frac{3}{8}$ in) to release the tension then sew the seam, using a straight stitch and keeping the flounce on top. Stitch slowly, ensuring both edges remain flat and keep accurately 1.5 cm ($\frac{3}{8}$ in) from the edge. Remove the basting. Trim the raw edge of the flounce to 2 mm ($\frac{1}{16}$ in). Trim the garment edge to 1 cm ($\frac{3}{8}$ in) and roll this edge over twice to cover the narrow edge. Baste with the fold on the machine stitching. Press the seam only with the tip of the iron. Hem the fold to the flounce, catching the machines stitches; on firm fabrics, machine with a wide zigzag stitch but without making a hard seam or it will impair the fall of the flounce. Remove the basting. Press lightly on RS if the fabric is suitable.

Hems

The choice of hem finish depends on the weight of the fabric, whether it is transparent, and also on the shape of the hemline, although exceptions can be made. For instance, you may decide to have a deep hem on a sheer fabric instead of a narrow one so that it provides a base for twin-needle stitching, embroidery, etc. Always allow shaped and circular pieces to hang for several days before trimming and turning up the hem. Use short lengths of perfectly matching thread for all hand-sewn hems.

Rolled and hand-sewn hem

This type of hem can be used on all except thick or stiff fabrics. You can hem transparent fabrics this way, also the shaped or circular edges of flounces, camisole hems, loose sleeves and tiers. A rolled hem would be suitable for the lower edge of a skirt in chiffon, georgette, etc., although it probably would not look absolutely straight when worn.

Trim the edge, leaving 5 mm ($\frac{1}{4}$ in) to turn up, slightly more on opaque fabrics that fray. If the fabric frays badly, mark the hemline but trim no more than 10 cm (4 in) at a time, stitching each section before trimming more. For the least visible finish, roll the raw edge to fold it over twice, hold the hem vertically and hem with very small stitches. An even narrower hem can be made by rolling the fabric and holding it horizontally but stitching with a loose oversewing stitch, working from left to right and taking the needle right over the folded edge. With both methods, moisten your fingers to get a grip on the raw edge to roll it tightly. On completion, press the hem very lightly. Flattening the fold often makes the hem stick out or look uneven.

Rolled and machine-sewn hem

This is suitable for most fabrics. Use on the edges of straight frills, straight or slightly shaped hems, sashes, straight necklines, sleeve edges and trouser hems. The finished width of the hem, and therefore the amount allowed for turning up, varies according to the thickness of the fabric. On fine silks, transparent fabrics, etc., trim the hem, leaving less than 1 cm ($\frac{3}{8}$ in) to turn up. On other fabrics leave 1 cm ($\frac{3}{8}$ in) or more.

Fold under a small amount and press either with the iron or by running the fold across the edge of the table, holding it taut. Place under the machine foot, fold the edge over again, lower the needle, lower the foot and stitch. Use a straight, zigzag or decorative stitch. Press.

Machine-rolled hem

The hemming foot on the machine can be used on fine fabrics, but it takes practice to hold the fabric and feed it into the foot correctly. Where possible, stitch the hem before joining the seams as the bulk may not pass evenly through the foot. Use this hem on the edges of frills, sleeves, jacket, long skirts, sashes and flounces, although it is not easy to stitch curved edges.

Attach the hemming foot or shell hem foot to the machine. Trim the edge of the fabric, leaving 5 mm ($\frac{1}{4}$ in) for the hem. Slot the end of the fabric into the foot and pull it out towards the back. Lower the foot and stitch, holding the raw edge upright and taut in front of the foot. Use a small straight stitch with the narrow hem foot, and a zigzag stitch with the shell hem foot. On completion, either cut off the end that is not hemmed or fold it and stitch it flat with the normal machine foot. Press.

Hairline hem

This hem is very quick to do. It is suitable for all sheer and soft fabrics, and other fabrics if they do not fray. Use it on hems, frill and flounce edges, and any long, straight runs.

Trim the fabric to 5 mm ($\frac{1}{4}$ in) longer than required. Put it under the machine foot, RS up, fold under the raw edge, lower the foot and stitch with a small zigzag stitch over the edge. Press the edge then carefully trim away the raw edge close to the stitching. Press again. For a more defined edge, zigzag a second time after trimming. For a corded edge, place fine crochet cotton or embroidery thread on the edge and zigzag over it. An alternative method, if you do not want to turn the edge under, is to machine a row of straight stitching on the hemline, trim off the fabric close to it then zigzag over the straight stitching. With chiffon and other fabrics that fray or give, it helps to put a row of straight stitching below the hemline before trimming the garment, in order to provide a firm edge to fold over.

Deep hand-sewn hem

Although this hem adds weight and improves the hang of a garment, it is not easy to do on slippery or transparent fabrics. In addition, the stitching may break after some wear which could present a hazard on long skirts and trousers. The effect of a deep hem is clumsy on very fine fabrics and on small garments such as camisoles, but it can be used for most other purposes. If you decide on a deep hem for weight but are not pleased with its appearance, you could add decorative stitching.

Mark the hemline. Fold up the hem and baste near the fold. Press. Trim away the surplus fabric, leaving sufficient to finish the hem. A straight or nearly straight hem may be 5–6 cm (2–2$\frac{1}{2}$ in) deep when finished. A shaped hem should not be more than 2.5 cm (1 in) deep when finished. Medium and heavy fabrics should be trimmed at that depth and zigzagged or overlocked before basting flat to the garment. On lightweight fabrics allow an additional 1 cm ($\frac{3}{8}$ in) and turn it under before basting it to the garment. If the fabric is springy, fold it under, baste the fold and press it before basting the hem to the garment.

Finish by slip hemming, picking up one thread from the garment and sliding the needle through the hem fold between stitches. Finish heavier hems by working catch stitch under the edge, still only picking up one thread on the needle and taking bigger stitches in the hem edge alternately. On fine fabrics, if you can see a shadow where the edge is folded under, allow more to turn under so that the raw edge reaches the basting at the fold.

Machined hem

Although the stitching can be seen, this is a safe hem for long dresses.

On all light- and medium-weight fabrics, mark, baste, press and fold the edge under as for the *Deep hand-sewn hem* above. On heavy fabrics, trim and zigzag the edge and baste the hem to the garment. With all fabrics, press the hem after basting and prepare to stitch, RS fabric uppermost.

The choice of stitch is very wide. Use decorative stitches, embroidery, twin needle, couching; you can even place a layer of wadding under the hem edge before basting, and achieve a quilted hem by adding lines of straight stitching. Some fabrics look best with a single row of stitching just below the hem edge, or even two rows, one below the edge and the other close to the lower fold. Experiment on spare fabric. Place Stitch 'n' Tear beneath the hem if it shows a tendency to pucker. Press all the stitching on completion, after removing the basting.

Adhesive web, e.g. Wundaweb

This method of securing a hem requires moisture and considerable iron pressure, so it is not suitable for fine, light, transparent or pile fabrics.

Mark the hemline, turn it up, baste near the fold and press. Trim the raw edge, leaving 3 cm ($1\frac{1}{8}$ in). Zigzag or overcast the edge. With the garment on the ironing board, place the Wundaweb or adhesive web under the hem edge, making sure the web is covered by the hem. Press the hem, covering it first with a damp pressing cloth until the adhesive has melted. Remove the basting and press again lightly.

3 Pattern Information and Variations

Full-Size Patterns

Strapless bodice

The panelled, fitted bodice is lined and supported with Rigilene polyester boning. The pattern pieces consist of a CF panel with a choice of neckline, a side front section, and a back pattern cut to a fold at CB. There is also an alternative gathered CF panel.

The zip is fitted in the left side seam where it is inconspicuous. If it is required at CB, the back pattern piece must be cut with a seam, first adding a seam allowance.

The basic front, side front and back patterns are used for making the lining, and also for a foundation bodice to be overlaid with a ruched bodice (diagram pattern).

Various straps and frills can be added.

A 1.5 cm ($\frac{5}{8}$ in) seam allowance is included on all edges.

Cutting out and making instructions are on page 72.

This pattern can easily be converted to a drop-waist bodice as follows. Lengthen all the pattern pieces by 11 cm ($4\frac{3}{8}$ in). At the new lower line add 3 cm ($1\frac{1}{4}$ in) to the side seams and curved front seams. Complete by drawing lines from the lower edge to join the original pattern edge. Draw the hem edge, keeping the original shape.

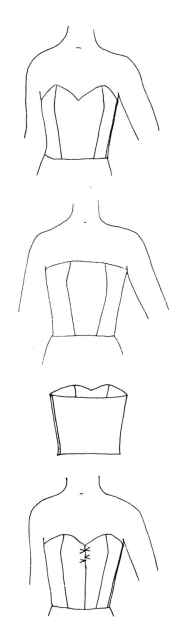

Fabric quantities
115 cm (45 in) wide
Strapless bodice (all sizes): 1 m ($1\frac{1}{4}$ yd)
Drop-waist bodice (all sizes): 1.60 m (2 yd)

Camisole

This semi-fitted strap top has a shaped upper edge, bust shaping coming from an underarm bust dart. The front and back are cut to the fold of the fabric. A zip goes into the left seam although if the pattern is made short and loose the zip can be omitted, especially if a knit fabric is used.

The camisole upper edge is finished with matching or contrast binding which also forms the straps (see measurements below).

The pattern pieces are cut to hip length, with alternative cutting

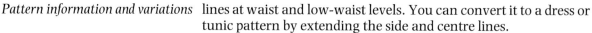

lines at waist and low-waist levels. You can convert it to a dress or tunic pattern by extending the side and centre lines.

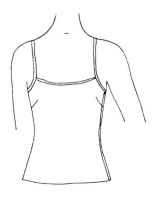

Lengthen the back and front 45 cm ($17\frac{5}{8}$ in) for below-knee length, and 87 cm ($34\frac{1}{4}$ in) for ankle length.

If you are binding the armhole, trim 1.5 cm ($\frac{5}{8}$ in) from the armhole edges and cut the binding 2.5 cm (1 in) wide to the following lengths:

Front upper binding:

Size		
12	28 cm	(11 in)
14	29 cm	($11\frac{1}{4}$ in)
16	29 cm	($11\frac{1}{4}$ in)
18	29 cm	($11\frac{1}{4}$ in)
20	30 cm	($11\frac{3}{4}$ in)

Back upper binding:

Size		
12	29 cm	($11\frac{1}{4}$ in)
14	29 cm	($11\frac{1}{4}$ in)
16	30 cm	($11\frac{3}{4}$ in)
18	30 cm	($11\frac{3}{4}$ in)
20	30 cm	($11\frac{3}{4}$ in)

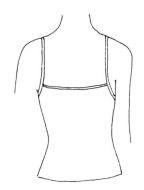

Armhole binding and shoulder strap (cut two):

Size		
12	62.5 cm	($24\frac{1}{2}$ in)
14	64.5 cm	($25\frac{1}{2}$ in)
16	66 cm	(26 in)
18	68 cm	($26\frac{3}{4}$ in)
20	70 cm	($27\frac{3}{4}$ in)

A 1.5 cm ($\frac{5}{8}$ in) seam or hem allowance is included on all edges.

Cutting out and making instructions are on page 89.

Fabric quantities

115 cm (45 in) wide

Hip length

Size		
12	1.40 m	($1\frac{2}{3}$ yd)
14	1.40 m	($1\frac{2}{3}$ yd)
16	1.40 m	($1\frac{2}{3}$ yd)
18	1.50 m	($1\frac{3}{4}$ yd)
20	1.50 m	($1\frac{3}{4}$ yd)

Below-knee length (all sizes): 2.50 m ($2\frac{3}{4}$ yd)

Ankle length (all sizes): 3.20 m ($3\frac{2}{3}$ yd)

Jacket

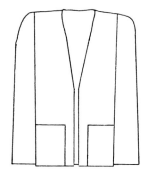

This simple, loose-fitting, edge-to-edge jacket has deep armholes and wide sleeves. It can also be made sleeveless. The back is cut to the fold of the fabric.

The pattern is cut to hip length, with alternative cutting lines below the waist and, for a bolero, above the waist. It can also be lengthened to knee or ankle length. The sleeve pattern is wrist length, with alternative seamlines and markings for a three-quarter sleeve with fold-back cuff.

The front edges can be finished with machine stitching or the jacket can be lined to the edge, using the same pattern pieces to cut the lining. There is also a pattern for a flounce to be attached to the necklines and front edge (diagram pattern, page 88).

From neck to hem, the pattern shown measures:

Size	12	14	16	18	20
Below waist	55 cm ($21\frac{5}{8}$ in)	55.5 cm ($21\frac{3}{4}$ in)	56 cm (22 in)	56.5 cm ($22\frac{1}{8}$ in)	57 cm ($22\frac{5}{8}$ in)
Hip length	68 cm ($26\frac{3}{4}$ in)	68.5 cm (27 in)	69 cm ($27\frac{1}{8}$ in)	69.5 cm ($27\frac{1}{4}$ in)	70 cm ($27\frac{1}{2}$ in)

To lengthen to mid-calf, extend the centre and side edges by 53 cm ($20\frac{3}{4}$ in). To lengthen to ankle length, add 81.5 cm ($32\frac{1}{8}$ in).

A 3 cm ($1\frac{1}{4}$ in) hem is allowed on all sizes and on the sleeve pattern. 1.5 cm ($\frac{5}{8}$ in) seams are allowed on all other edges.

Cutting out and making instructions are on page 87.

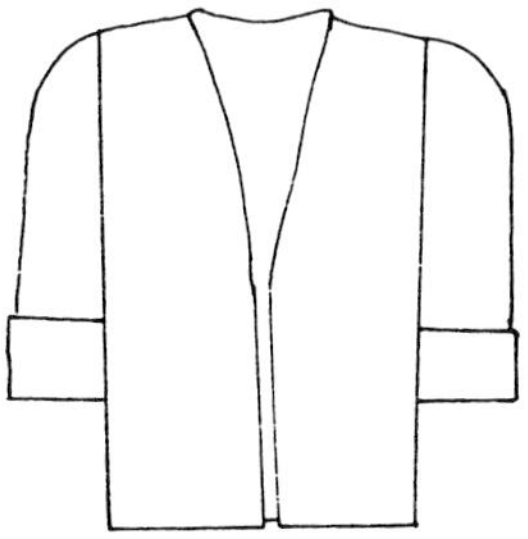

Pocket pattern

Cut two 21.5 cm × 20 cm ($8\frac{1}{2}$ in × 8 in), and turn a 3 cm ($1\frac{1}{4}$ in) hem on the upper edge. Place the lower edge of the pocket to the finished edge of the hip-length jacket, 10 cm (4 in) from the finished front edge.

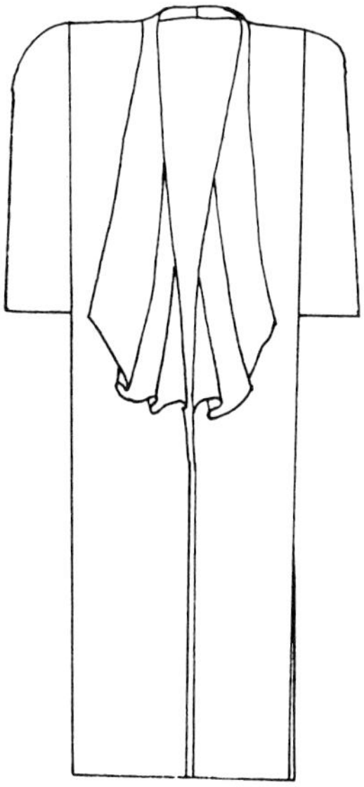

Fabric quantities

115 cm (45 in) wide

Jacket, below waist plus flounce:

Size	12	2.80 m ($3\frac{1}{4}$ yd)
	14	2.80 m ($3\frac{1}{4}$ yd)
	16	2.90 m ($3\frac{1}{3}$ yd)
	18	3 m ($3\frac{1}{3}$ yd)
	20	3 m ($3\frac{1}{3}$ yd)

Ankle length plus flounce and pockets:

Size	12	4.60 m ($5\frac{1}{4}$ yd)
	14	4.60 m ($5\frac{1}{4}$ yd)
	16	4.80 m ($5\frac{1}{3}$ yd)
	18	4.90 m ($5\frac{1}{2}$ yd)
	20	4.90 m ($5\frac{1}{2}$ yd)

Hip length plus flounce and pockets:

Size	12	2.90 m ($3\frac{1}{3}$ yd)
	14	3 m ($3\frac{1}{3}$ yd)
	16	3.20 m ($3\frac{2}{3}$ yd)
	18	3.20 m ($3\frac{2}{3}$ yd)
	20	3.30 m ($3\frac{3}{4}$ yd)

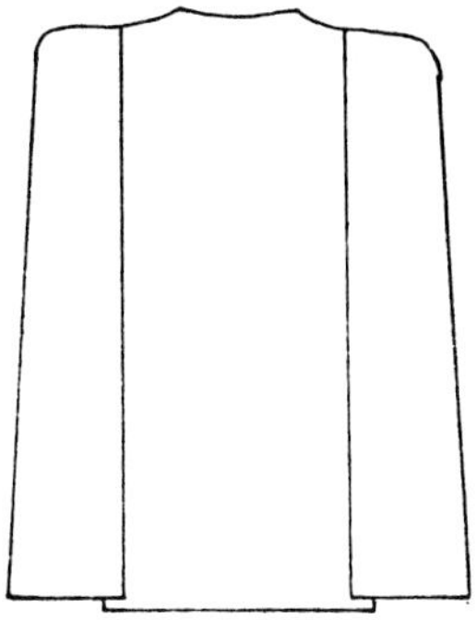

Mid-calf length plus flounce and pockets:

Size	12	4 m ($4\frac{1}{2}$ yd)
	14	4.10 m ($4\frac{2}{3}$ yd)
	16	4.30 m ($4\frac{3}{4}$ yd)
	18	4.30 m ($4\frac{3}{4}$ yd)
	20	4.40 m (5 yd)

Flounce only:

All sizes: 90 cm (1 yd)

Cap-sleeve top

A simple but versatile pattern, this top can have a variety of necklines. It has an alternative cut-away armhole. One pattern

Pattern information and variations piece is used for both front and back, placed to the fold of the fabric. The pattern is cut to hip length.

The necklines are round, V and low-scoop shape, and any of these can be used for front and back. The top can be lined to the neck and armhole, using the same pattern piece to cut the lining, or the neckline can be bound with 2.5 cm (1 in) wide bias strips cut to the following lengths:

Round neck (front and back):

Size	
12	65 cm (25½ in)
14	67 cm (26⅜ in)
16	67 cm (26⅜ in)
18	69 cm (27⅛ in)
20	70 cm (28 in)

Scoop neck (front) and round neck (back):

Size	
12	78 cm (30¾ in)
14	81 cm (31¾ in)
16	82 cm (32¼ in)
18	85 cm (33½ in)
20	86 cm (33¾ in)

V-neck (front) and round neck (back):

Size	
12	85 cm (33½ in)
14	87 cm (34¼ in)
16	90 cm (35½ in)
18	92 cm (36¼ in)
20	95 cm (37⅜ in)

The cut-away armhole is also bound with 2.5 cm (1 in) wide bias strips:

Size	
12	70 cm (28 in)
14	70 cm (28 in)
16	75 cm (30 in)
18	80 cm (32 in)
20	80 cm (32 in)

A 1.5 cm (⅝ in) seam allowance is included on all edges.

Cutting out and making instructions are on page 79.

The pattern can be lengthened and used for a dress or overdress by extending the centre and side edges as follows:
below-knee dress: lengthen by 45 cm (17¾ in)
ankle-length dress: lengthen by 87 cm (34¼ in)
tunic: lengthen by 32 cm (12½ in)

Fabric quantities
115 cm (45 in) wide

Cap-sleeve blouse, round neck:

Size	
12	1.80 m (2 yd)
14	1.80 m (2 yd)
16	1.90 m (2¼ yd)
18	1.90 m (2¼ yd)
20	1.90 m (2¼ yd)

Blouse, V-neck and flounce:

Size	
12	2 m (2⅓ yd)
14	2 m (2⅓ yd)
16	2 m (2⅓ yd)
18	2.10 m (2⅓ yd)
20	2.20 m (2½ yd)

Below knee, round neck:

Size		
12	2.70 m	(3¼ yd)
14	2.70 m	(3¼ yd)
16	2.80 m	(3¼ yd)
18	2.80 m	(3¼ yd)
20	2.80 m	(3¼ yd)

Ankle length, round neck:

Size		
12	3.50 m	(4 yd)
14	3.50 m	(4 yd)
16	3.60 m	(4¼ yd)
18	3.70 m	(4¼ yd)
20	3.70 m	(4¼ yd)

Tunic, round neck:

Size		
12	2.40 m	(2¾ yd)
14	2.40 m	(2¾ yd)
16	2.50 m	(3 yd)
18	2.60 m	(3¼ yd)
20	2.60 m	(3¼ yd)

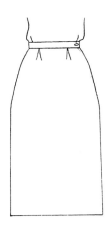

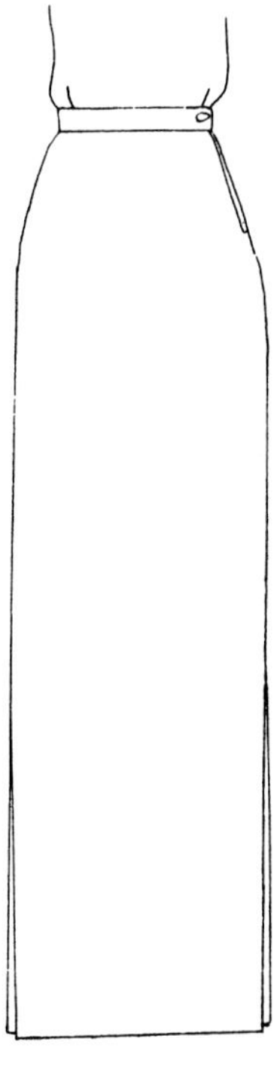

Skirt

This straight skirt pattern is fitted with darts at the back waist and folded tucks at the front. The back and front are cut to the fold of the fabric, and the zip is inserted in the left side seam.

The pattern is cut to hip level. It can be used as it is with a straight gathered skirt attached, or it can be lengthened to above or below the knee, or to ankle length, by extending the centre and side edges.

Cut the waistband 19 cm (7½ in) wide to the following lengths and cut Fold-a-Band, petersham or other waist stiffening the same length:

Size	
12	75.5 cm (29¾ in)
14	78.5 cm (31 in)
16	84 cm (33 in)
18	87.5 cm (34½ in)
20	92.5 cm (36¾ in)

This allows 2.5 cm (1 in) overlap.

Fold the tucks towards CF when attaching the waistband.

Lengthen the pattern as follows if required:

short length: add 28 cm (11 in)
below-knee length: add 45 cm (17¾ in)
mid-calf length: add 58 cm (22¾ in)
ankle length: add 87 cm (34¼ in)

A 3 cm (1¼ in) hem is included. 1.5 cm (⅝ in) seams are allowed on all other edges.

Cutting out and making instructions are on page 80.

Fabric quantities

115 cm (45 in) wide
Short length:

Size	
12	90 cm (1 yd)
14	90 cm (1 yd)
16	1.20 m (1½ yd)
18	1.20 m (1½ yd)
20	1.20 m (1½ yd)

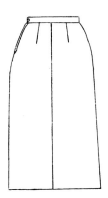

Pattern information and variations

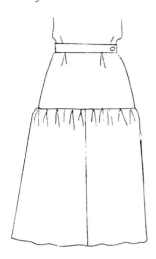

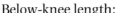

Below-knee length:

Size		
12	90 cm (1 yd)	
14	90 cm (1 yd)	
16	1.60 m ($1\frac{3}{4}$ yd)	
18	1.60 m ($1\frac{3}{4}$ yd)	
20	1.60 m ($1\frac{3}{4}$ yd)	

Ankle length:

Size		
12	1.40 m ($1\frac{2}{3}$ yd)	
14	1.40 m ($1\frac{2}{3}$ yd)	
16	2.50 m (3 yd)	
18	2.50 m (3 yd)	
20	2.50 m (3 yd)	

Trousers

The straight-legged, pull-on trousers are cut in one piece without side seams. The waist edge folds over to form a casing for the elastic. One pattern piece is provided, cut to 14 cm ($5\frac{1}{2}$ in) below crutch level. Lengthen the pattern as follows:

(a) Extend line A:

Size	
12	59.5 cm ($23\frac{1}{2}$ in)
14	60 cm ($23\frac{1}{2}$ in)
16	61 cm (24 in)
18	61.5 cm ($24\frac{1}{4}$ in)
20	62 cm ($24\frac{3}{8}$ in)

(b) Rule a horizontal line at 45 degrees at the bottom of line A. Extend this line 26.5 cm ($10\frac{1}{2}$ in) in each direction. Extend the inner leg lines to meet these points.

(c) To make the hem, draw a line below this 3 cm ($1\frac{1}{4}$ in) from it. Fold the paper along the upper line and cut the sides to form shaped seam edges.

The finished length of the trousers is:

Size	
12	106 cm ($41\frac{3}{4}$ in)
14	107 cm (42 in)
16	108 cm ($42\frac{1}{2}$ in)
18	108.5 cm ($42\frac{3}{4}$ in)
20	109 cm (43 in)

A 3 cm ($1\frac{1}{4}$ in) hem is included, and 3 cm ($1\frac{1}{4}$ in) is allowed at the waist for the casing. A 1.5 cm ($\frac{5}{8}$ in) seam allowance is allowed on other edges.

Use 2.5 cm (1 in) elastic.

Cutting out and making instructions are on page 82.

Fabric quantities

Size	
12	2.50 m (3 yd)
14	2.50 m (3 yd)
16	2.50 m (3 yd)
18	2.50 m (3 yd)
20	2.60 m ($3\frac{1}{4}$ yd)

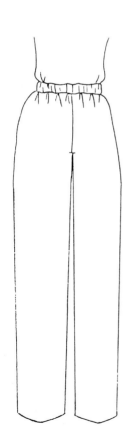

Big puff sleeve

Designed to be made in matching or contrast fabric and inserted in the camisole armhole, this sleeve has elastic through the hem. It can be cut above or below elbow level, or you could make it wrist length by adding 17.5 cm ($6\frac{3}{4}$ in) to the hem. The underarm section is attached to the camisole and the remainder of the sleeve head is gathered and bound. Alternatively, neaten the raw edge and insert several rows of shirring elastic until its size is sufficiently reduced.

A 2 cm ($\frac{3}{4}$ in) hem is allowed on the upper and lower edges, and a 1.5 cm ($\frac{5}{8}$ in) seam is allowed on the sleeve.

Fabric quantity
90 cm (36 in) or 115 cm (45 in) wide: 60 cm ($\frac{2}{3}$ yd), for each sleeve

Haberdashery
Thread; narrow elastic for lower arm; narrow elastic or shirring elastic for sleeve head (optional)

Cutting out
1 or 2 sleeves, to length required, with SG as pattern *or* on striped or check fabric, at 45 degrees

Sewing
1. Snip the sleeve edge to the dot on the pattern. If the fabric frays, press a small square of light iron-on Vilene over the dot on WS before cutting. Fold the edge of the sleeve head 2 cm ($\frac{3}{4}$ in) to WS, turn under to make a hem and stitch along the fold. Fasten off the ends securely.
2. Fold the sleeve WS out, stitch the seam, neaten the edges and press. If you are using chiffon or other transparent fabric, make French or narrow seams.
3. Turn up and stitch a 2 cm ($\frac{3}{4}$ in) hem along the lower edge, leaving space in the stitching for the elastic. Measure the elastic round your arm, add 1 cm ($\frac{3}{8}$ in) for the join and thread it through the hem. Overlap the ends of the elastic and stitch, then complete the stitching along the hem fold.
4. Complete the camisole except for the armhole edge and finish the neck edge with binding. Matching underarm seams, attach the sleeve to the armhole with RS together and raw edges level. Make sure the edge of the camisole is level with the end of the sleeve head hem. Stitch the armhole seam, trim and neaten.
5. Draw up the sleeve head to fit the shoulder by one of the following methods:
(a) Measure the elastic approximately, thread it through the hem and secure one end firmly by stitching across the hem at least twice. Put on the dress, pull up the elastic and pin. Trim and secure the ends as before.
(b) Omit stage 1 of the sleeve construction (making the sleeve head hem) but make and attach the sleeve as described. Insert two gathering threads over the sleeve head a little less than 2 cm ($\frac{3}{4}$ in) inside the edge. Pull up these threads and secure them by winding them round a pin. Even out the gathers. Try on the dress and tighten or loosen the gathers to fit the shoulder. Cut bias strips of fabric 2.5 cm (1 in) wide and the length of the gathered edge plus 3 cm ($1\frac{1}{4}$ in). Attach the binding to RS sleeve, stitching just below the gathering thread and level with the armhole seam stitching. Fold in the ends of the binding to the inside, fold in the raw edge of

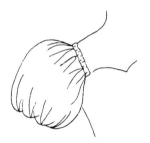

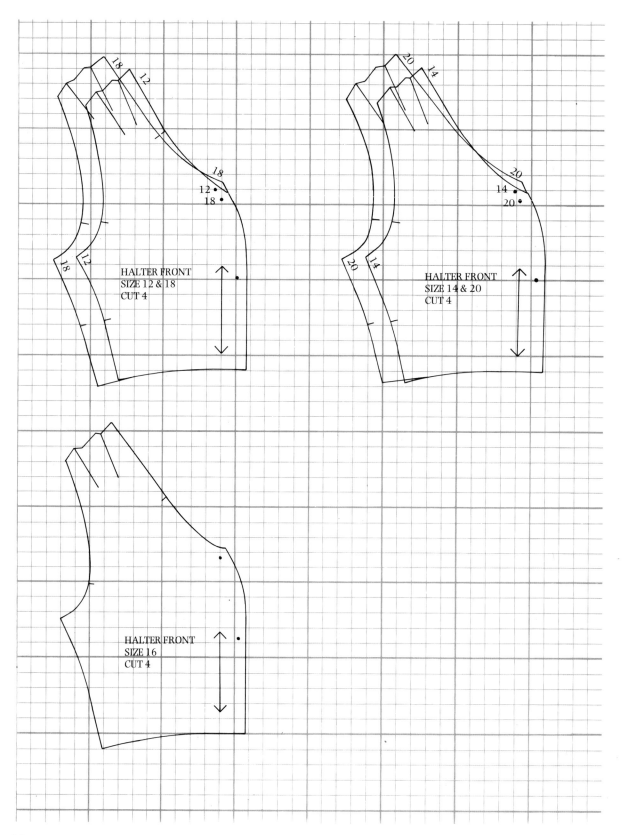

HALTER FRONT
SIZE 12 & 18
CUT 4

HALTER FRONT
SIZE 14 & 20
CUT 4

HALTER FRONT
SIZE 16
CUT 4

40

the binding, roll it to WS and baste in place over the gathers. Finish by hemming along the fold of the binding and stitching the ends of the binding together. Pull the thread tight to gather the binding and stitch it to the end of the binding on the camisole neckline.

Diagram Patterns

These are shown on a grid. Each square represents 2.5 cm (1 in).

Halter top

A waist-length top lined with self fabric or lining, this has a gathered front seam and pleats at the shoulder. The back neck strap is a tube of fabric with elastic through it. The front pattern only is in diagram form, and has been designed to be used with the back of the strapless bodice pattern. This should also be lined, and can be boned if required. The halter fastens with hooks and eyes on tape stitched to the left side seam.

To make the strap pattern, cut paper 4.6 cm (1¾ in) wide with the length as follows:

Size	12	24.5 cm (9⅝ in)
	14	24.5 cm (9⅝ in)
	16	25.5 cm (10 in)
	18	26.5 cm (10 in)
	20	26.5 cm (10 in)

The strap will hold elastic 13 mm (½ in) wide. There is a 1.5 cm (⅝ in) seam allowance throughout.

Cutting out and making instructions are on page 82.

Fabric quantity
115 cm (45 in) wide
All sizes: 1.20 m (1½ yd)
Lining: as above

Waterfall overskirt

A one-size pattern for a circular floating skirt section, this can be cut twice, bound along the waist edge and worn separately over a skirt. Alternatively, as a front only, the straight edge can be included with the stitching of the waist and side seam of the skirt.

There is a 1.5 cm (⅝ in) seam allowance on the long edge and the waist; elsewhere the seams are 1 cm (⅜ in).

Fabric quantity
115 cm (45 in) wide: 1.60 m (2 yd) single panel, 2.40 m (2⅔ yd) double panel

Haberdashery
Thread

Cutting out (single panel)
1 × skirt, with pattern RS up on RS fabric *or* draw shape of pattern on RS fabric, using tailor's chalk or fabric pen.

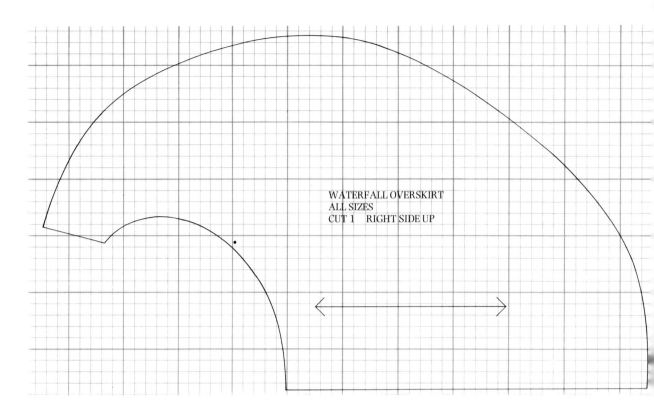

WATERFALL OVERSKIRT
ALL SIZES
CUT 1   RIGHT SIDE UP

Sewing (single panel)
1. Roll a narrow hem along the short straight edge and stitch. Roll another narrow hem along the circular edge and stitch. This can be done using the narrow hemming foot on the machine, or it can be hemmed by hand or machined with a decorative stitch. Press.
2. Cut out the front skirt of the dress and spread RS up. Place the floating panel on top WS down, matching the waist edges; ease the panel onto the dress. Match the raw edge of the panel to the side edge of the skirt. Baste along the seam and waist. Complete the dress.

Cutting out (double panel)
Fold the fabric RS out, place the pattern in position and cut out.

Sewing (double panel)
1. With RS together, stitch, trim and neaten the long seam.
2. Roll a narrow hem along both short edges and stitch. Roll and stitch a narrow hem around the circular edge of the skirt. Press.
3. Cut and join bias strips of fabric 2.5 cm (1 in) wide to waist size, plus two tie ends of about 40 cm (16 in) each. Pass the strip through a tape maker and press. Fold the strip and press in half to mark the centre.
    Mark off the waist size in the centre of the strip.
4. Apply the bias strip to the skirt waist with RS strip to RS skirt, taking a 1.5 cm ($\frac{5}{8}$ in) seam on the skirt. Match the centre mark on

the bias strip to the seam, and the dot on the pattern to CF and CB.
Stitch along the skirt waist in the crease of the bias strip. Trim the raw edges. Fold in the ends of the binding, then fold the binding until the edges meet along the tie ends and the fold falls on the stitching line of the waist. Baste and press. Stitch close to the edge of the strip from end to end, including across the waist.

Triangular top

This loose-fitting top is worn over one shoulder as a cover-up on top of a dress or blouse. It has one side seam, tucks in the shoulder seam, and elastic through the waistline to hold it in place.

There is a 1.5 cm ($\frac{5}{8}$ in) seam allowance at the side and shoulder, and 1 cm ($\frac{3}{8}$ in) elsewhere.

Making instructions are on page 94.

Fabric quantity
115 cm (45 in) wide: 1.90 m ($2\frac{1}{3}$ yd), including a belt

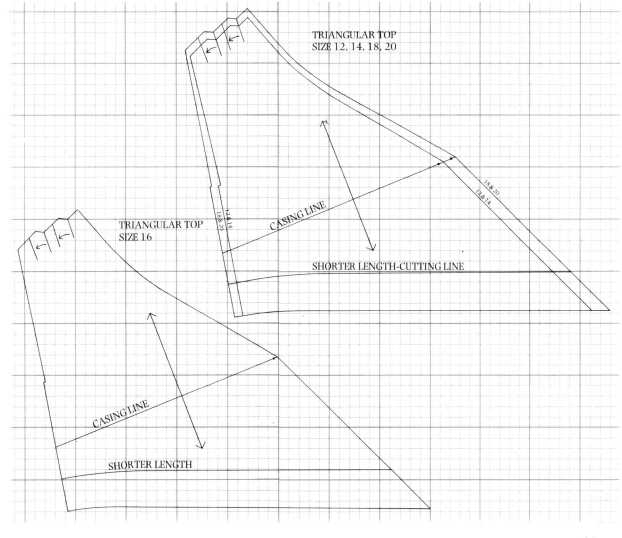

TRIANGULAR TOP
SIZE 12, 14, 18, 20

TRIANGULAR TOP
SIZE 16

CASING LINE

CASING LINE

SHORTER LENGTH-CUTTING LINE

SHORTER LENGTH

18 & 20

12 & 14

Shaped sleeve

A below-elbow sleeve with full gathered head and fitted lower edge, this can be attached to the camisole, stitching the underarm of the sleeve to the armhole. The sleeve head is hemmed and pulled up to fit, using elastic. The lower edge of the sleeve may be faced or bound.

There is a 1.5 cm ($\frac{5}{8}$ in) allowance on the seam; 1 cm ($\frac{3}{8}$ in) on the hem; and 2 cm ($1\frac{1}{4}$ in) on the sleeve head.

Fabric quantity
115 cm (45 in) wide: 1.10 m ($1\frac{1}{3}$ yd)

Haberdashery
Thread; narrow elastic, for the sleeve head

Cutting out
2 × sleeve: place pattern, drawn to size, on double fabric
2 × 3 cm ($1\frac{1}{4}$ in) bias strips, to fit the lower edge of the sleeve

Sewing
1. With RS together, apply each bias strip to the lower edge of each sleeve, taking 1 cm ($\frac{3}{8}$ in) seam on the sleeve and 6 mm ($\frac{1}{4}$ in) on the strip. Stitch, then snip along the curve and trim the raw edges. For a visible finish, fold in the raw edge of the strip, roll to WS sleeve and hem or machine, with the fold resting on the machine stitches. For a faced finish, roll the strip completely to WS, roll and press the edge and finish the outer edge of the strip by turning under and hemming.
2. Snip the edge of the sleeve head to the dot on the pattern. Fold the edge 2 cm ($\frac{3}{4}$ in) to WS, fold under to form a hem and stitch along the fold.

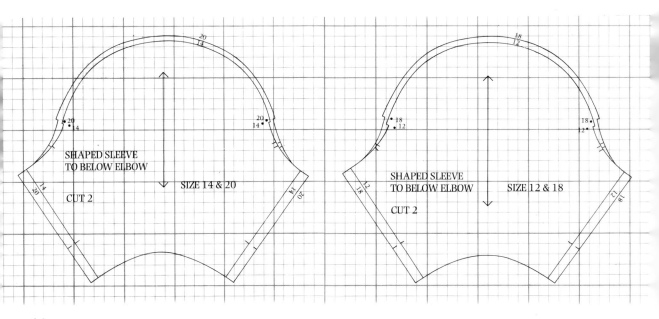

SHAPED SLEEVE
TO BELOW ELBOW

SIZE 14 & 20

CUT 2

SHAPED SLEEVE
TO BELOW ELBOW

SIZE 12 & 18

CUT 2

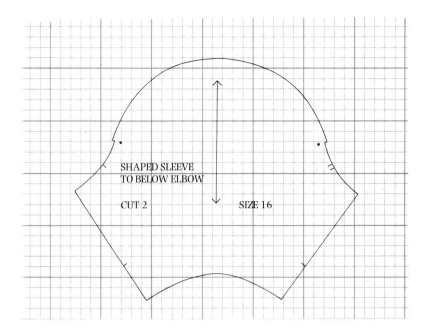

SHAPED SLEEVE
TO BELOW ELBOW

CUT 2   SIZE 16

3. Fold the sleeve WS out and stitch the underarm seam, matching the hem edges precisely. Trim 3 mm ($\frac{1}{8}$ in) off the raw edges and neaten. Press.

4. Complete the camisole except for the armhole, finishing the neck edge with binding. Match the underarm seams of the sleeve and bodice, place RS together and baste. Make sure the end of the sleeve head hem meets the upper edge of the camisole. Stitch the seam, trim and neaten.

5. Measure the elastic approximately and thread it through the sleeve head. Secure one end by stitching across the hem at least twice. Put on the garment and adjust the elastic to fit. Trim the end and stitch the elastic as before.

Two-piece gathered sleeve

This shaped sleeve is gathered over the head and along a central seam, and fitted at above-elbow level.

1.5 cm ($\frac{5}{8}$ in) is allowed on the seams; 1 cm ($\frac{3}{8}$ in) at the hem; and 2 cm ($\frac{3}{4}$ in) over the sleeve head.

Fabric quantities
115 cm (45 in) wide:

Size		
	12	1 m ($1\frac{1}{4}$ yd)
	14	1 m ($1\frac{1}{4}$ yd)
	16	1.10 m ($1\frac{1}{3}$ yd)
	18	1.10 m ($1\frac{1}{3}$ yd)
	20	1.10 m ($1\frac{1}{3}$ yd)

Haberdashery
Thread; narrow elastic, for the sleeve head

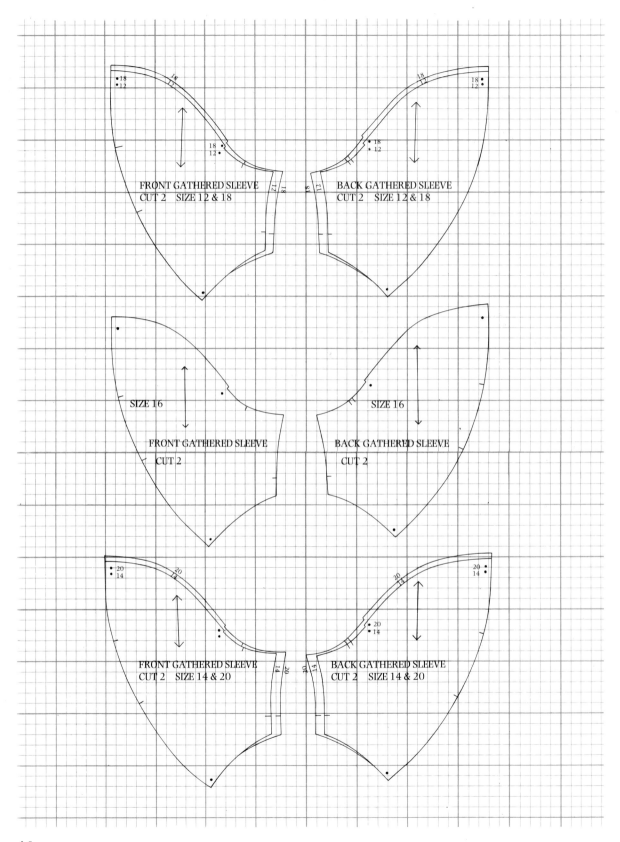

FRONT GATHERED SLEEVE
CUT 2   SIZE 12 & 18

BACK GATHERED SLEEVE
CUT 2   SIZE 12 & 18

SIZE 16

SIZE 16

FRONT GATHERED SLEEVE

CUT 2

BACK GATHERED SLEEVE

CUT 2

FRONT GATHERED SLEEVE
CUT 2   SIZE 14 & 20

BACK GATHERED SLEEVE
CUT 2   SIZE 14 & 20

46

Cutting out

2 × back sleeve, 2 × front sleeve

2 × 3 cm (1¼ in) bias strips, to fit the lower edge of the sleeve

Sewing

1. With back and front sleeve RS together, insert the gathering thread along the curved seam. Pull up the thread until the seam is reduced to 36 cm (14 in). Tie the thread ends. Even out the gathers and stitch the seam. Trim the raw edges and neaten both together. Open out the sleeve and pull hard against the seam to separate the gathers and reveal the seam on RS.

2. Bind or face the sleeve hem. Attach the sleeve to the camisole and finish the sleeve head, following instructions 1–5 on page 44.

Flounce for jacket neckline

This bias-cut triangular pattern has a seam at CB of the neck. It is made in single fabric and is attached to the jacket neckline and partway down the front edge, using a bias strip or flat fell seam.

There is a 1.5 cm (⅝ in) seam allowance.

Cutting out and making instructions are on page 88.

Fabric quantity

115 cm (45 in): 90 cm (1 yd)

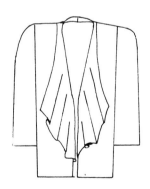

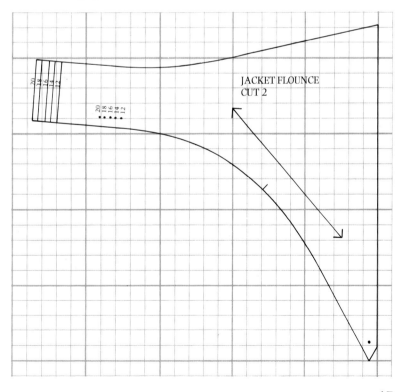

JACKET FLOUNCE
CUT 2

Pattern information and variations

Ruched bodice

A strapless, boned bodice fitted to below the waist, this consists of a CF panel, a side front panel and a back bodice. The fabric is gathered along all the seams. The bodice fastens at the left side with a zip if it is attached to a skirt, or with hooks and eyes on tape if it is not.

There is a 1.5 cm ($\frac{5}{8}$ in) seam allowance.

Use the pattern pieces from the strapless bodice (full-size pattern) as a lining, or as a base if the ruched bodice is to be made in transparent fabric. Fabric quantities, and cutting out and making instructions are on page 106.

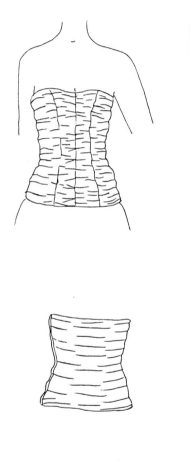

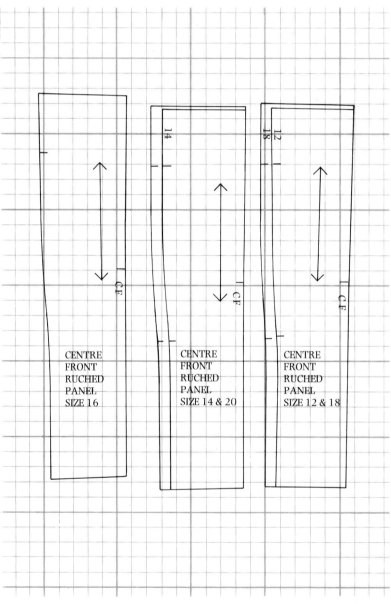

CENTRE FRONT RUCHED PANEL SIZE 16

CENTRE FRONT RUCHED PANEL SIZE 14 & 20

CENTRE FRONT RUCHED PANEL SIZE 12 & 18

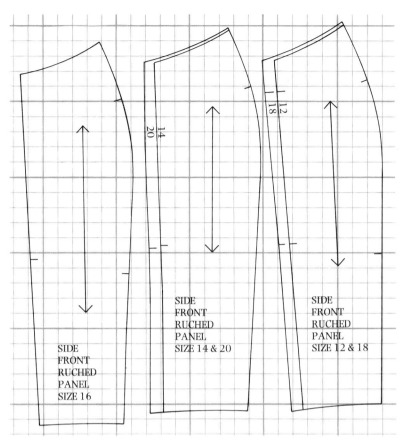

SIDE
FRONT
RUCHED
PANEL
SIZE 16

SIDE
FRONT
RUCHED
PANEL
SIZE 14 & 20

SIDE
FRONT
RUCHED
PANEL
SIZE 12 & 18

Patterns from Measurements

Some of these are one size, some give different measurements for
each size. All the shapes are simple to draw.

Circular skirts

A circular skirt is a full circle of fabric that can be made to ankle or
mid-calf length or to mini-length. The same shape can also be used
very short as a waist peplum, worn as an accessory or attached to
a strapless bodice. Another alternative is to use the same principle
to make a circular flounce to attach to a dress hemline.

The pattern is a very easy one to make, and if you are sure of
your measurements it can be cut directly in fabric. The position of
the seams in the skirt depends on the width of the fabric used. A
small circle can be cut without any seams, from fabric folded into
four. With most skirts, you will have to cut two half-circles and
make two seams to be positioned as side seams. Few fabrics are
wide enough to cut an ankle-length circular skirt without joins
above the hem. To do this, begin by cutting the two half-circles
and then, using the surplus fabric, make a join along SG to add
enough fabric to complete the circle full length.

To make a circular pattern, draw a quarter circle as described

Pattern information and variations below. The resulting waist measurement makes a skirt that will fit the waist of the strapless bodice. If you are only making a skirt, ease this shape onto the waistband. The waist edge, or the arc of a flounce, will stretch easily with excessive handling. If you have not made circular pattern shapes before, you will find it easier to make the arc longer than described and to gather the edge to fit the remainder of the garment. This means lowering the line shown on the illustration, and adjusting the length from that point to the hem accordingly.

There is a 1.5 cm ($\frac{5}{8}$ in) seam allowance on the seams and hem.
Finished length of ankle-length skirt: 108 cm ($42\frac{1}{2}$ in)
Finished length of mid-calf skirt: 80 cm ($31\frac{1}{2}$ in)

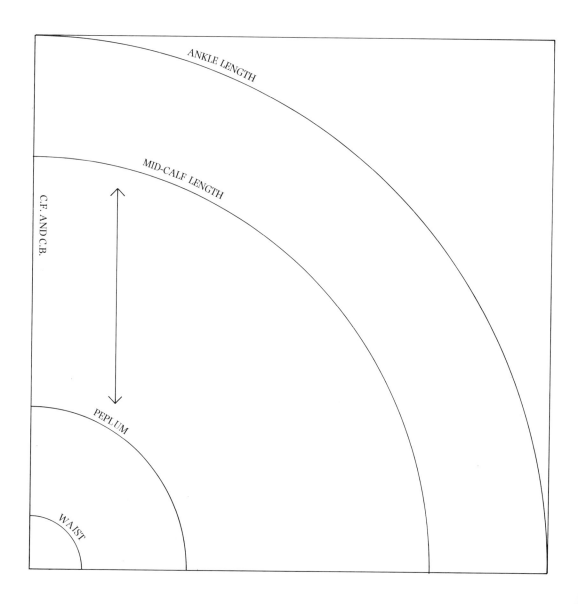

Drawing the pattern

Draw a square on paper, or use tailor's chalk on the fabric, with sides the following size:

(a) ankle length

Size		
12	123 cm	($48\frac{1}{2}$ in)
14	123.5 cm	($48\frac{3}{4}$ in)
16	124.3 cm	(49 in)
18	125 cm	($49\frac{1}{8}$ in)
20	125.5 cm	($49\frac{1}{2}$ in)

(b) mid-calf length

Size		
12	95 cm	($37\frac{3}{8}$ in)
14	95.5 cm	($37\frac{1}{2}$ in)
16	96.3 cm	($37\frac{3}{4}$ in)
18	97 cm	($38\frac{1}{8}$ in)
20	97.5 cm	($38\frac{1}{2}$ in)

(c) peplum

Size		
12	37 cm	($14\frac{1}{2}$ in)
14	37.5 cm	($14\frac{3}{4}$ in)
16	38.3 cm	($15\frac{1}{8}$ in)
18	39 cm	($15\frac{1}{4}$ in)
20	39.5 cm	($15\frac{1}{2}$ in)

(d) mini

Somewhere between peplum and mid-calf, depending on preference. Assess the size of square required.

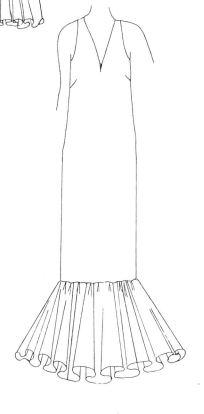

At one corner of the square, draw a quarter circle for the waist with a radius as follows:

Size		
12	12 cm	($4\frac{3}{4}$ in)
14	12.5 cm	($4\frac{7}{8}$ in)
16	13.3 cm	($5\frac{1}{4}$ in)
18	14 cm	($5\frac{1}{2}$ in)
20	14.5 cm	($5\frac{3}{4}$ in)

From the same corner, draw a quarter circle with a radius the same length as the sides of the square.

These quarter circle arcs can be easily and accurately drawn using a tape measure. Measure carefully and repeatedly, making short marks with pencil or, on fabric, with tailor's chalk. Alternatively, cut a piece of string to the required length, attach the pencil to the end and swing it from the corner.

Note the position of SG. If you have made a pattern in paper, mark CF and CB and the size, and mark it 'Cut two to a fold'.

Making instructions are on page 72.

Circular hemline flounce

This deep circle of fabric can be attached to the hemline of the mid-calf camisole dress. It is made of six pieces of fabric.

First mark a quarter-circle with a radius of 56 cm (22 in). Then mark an inner semi-circle with a radius of 13 cm ($5\frac{1}{4}$ in). SG should be parallel to the straight edge. Cut six.

1.5 cm ($\frac{5}{8}$ in) is allowed on the seams and hem, for ease of

handling. Allowance has been made for some gathering when attaching the flounce to the dress.

Making instructions are on page 84.

Circular neckline flounce

Circles of fabric are joined and attached to the V-neck of the cap-sleeve pattern. Consisting of six pieces of fabric, the size allows for a V at the back (or front) and a round neck at the front (or back).

Mark a full circle with a radius of 13 cm ($5\frac{1}{4}$ in) and an inner circle with a radius of 3 cm ($1\frac{1}{4}$ in). Cut six in fabric then cut along the radius of each one.

1.5 cm ($\frac{5}{8}$ in) seams are allowed for joining the circles together and attaching them to the backing. There is a hem of 1 cm ($\frac{3}{8}$ in). Allowance has been made for slight gathering when attaching the flounce. See page 36 for the length of the neckline binding used to attach the flounce.

Making instructions are on page 78.

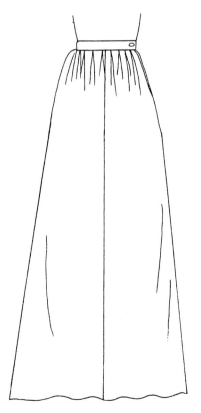

Gathered skirts

This pattern produces a flared and gathered skirt that can be any length. It can be attached to the waist or drop waist of the strapless top, camisole or skirt, or it can be gathered to fit a straight or shaped waistband. I suggest you make a paper pattern as described below, marking all the lengths, so that whatever version is required it can simply be traced off.

Cut a rectangle of paper 92 cm × 115 cm (36 in × $45\frac{1}{4}$ in). Fold lengthways. Measure from the fold along the upper edge 18.3 cm ($7\frac{1}{4}$ in). Rule a line from this point to the bottom corner. This is the

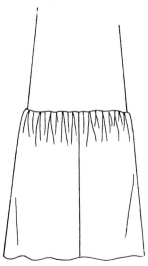

seam edge of the panel. At the waist, measure along the fold
2.5 cm (1 in). Draw a curve from this point up to the top of the
seamline.

GATHERED SKIRT

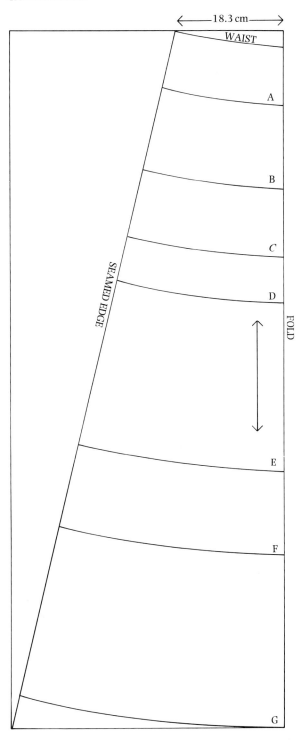

To mark the various hemlines, measure evenly along the fold and along the seamline as follows, and draw curved lines:

(a) cutting line for a drop waist: 9.6 cm (3¾ in) below the waistline

(b) placement line for attaching the middle tier of a drop-waist tiered skirt: 23.5 cm (9¼ in)

(c) placement line for attaching the middle tier of an ankle-length skirt: 34 cm (13⅜ in)

(d) cutting line for a drop-waist tiered skirt: 42.5 cm (16¾ in)

(e) cutting line for below-knee length, also for attaching a deep frill: 70 cm (27½ in)

(f) hemline for a mid-calf skirt: 84.5 cm (33¼ in)

(g) hemline for an ankle-length skirt: 112.5 cm (44 in)

For all versions, open out the pattern and cut four times, with SG along the centre of the pattern.

There is a 1.5 cm (⅝ in) seam and hem allowance.

Fabric quantities
115 cm (45 in) wide (all sizes)
below-knee length: 3.10 m (3½ yd)
mid-calf length: 3.70 m (4¼ yd)
ankle length: 4.80 m (5⅓ yd)

Sewing
Join all four seams, leaving the top of one seam open 20 cm (8 in). Then proceed as for individual versions in Chapter 4.

Ankle-length frilled skirt

This long gathered skirt has a deep frill applied to the hem.

Trace the pattern to hemline E. For the frill, cut six pieces 90 cm × 48.5 cm (36 in × 19¼ in).

There is a 1.5 cm (⅝ in) seam and hem allowance. 4 cm (1½ in) is allowed at the upper edge to make a frilled edge on RS.

Fabric quantity
115 cm (45 in) wide: 6 m (6½ yd)

Haberdashery
Thread; 20 cm (8 in) zip for the skirt *or* 40 cm (16 in) zip for the strapless dress; Wundaweb, if required, for the frilled hem

Cutting out
2 × back skirt panels; 2 × front skirt panels; 6 × frill pieces

Sewing
1. Join the frill pieces together. Press the seams. Turn up and stitch the hem along the lower edge. Alternatively, neaten the raw edge, press to WS and secure with Wundaweb.

2. At the upper edge of the frill, neaten the raw edge, fold 2.5 cm (1 in) to WS and press. Divide the frill into eight and insert eight gathering threads, one in each section, 2 cm ($\frac{3}{4}$ in) below the fold.
3. Neaten the lower edge of the skirt and divide the edge into eight. Overlap the upper edge of the frill onto the skirt, both RS up, taking 1.5 cm ($\frac{5}{8}$ in) seam allowance on the skirt. Pin the gathering line to the seamline of the skirt, matching the eight points. Working on one section at a time, pull up each gathering thread until the frill lies flat on the skirt. Fasten off the end of the thread and even out the gathers. Pin each section and baste, then move on to the next section.

Stitch the frill to the skirt; machine with RS up and following the gathering line. A small-size zigzag stitch works quite well as it conceals the gathering thread. Alternatively, zigzag over a thick yarn or glitter thread. Remove the basting and press the skirt. Gather the waist to fit a bodice or attach the skirt to a waistband.

Check the length of the skirt and lift it at the waist if necessary.

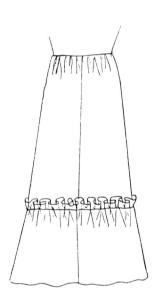

Ankle-length layered skirt

You can attach this skirt to the strapless top or make it as a skirt. It can be made from three complete gathered skirts, one cut to hemline, B, one to E, and one to G.

If you do not want so much bulk, make one skirt and add frills to attach in three layers. Trace the gathered skirt pattern to length E.
Bottom layer: cut five pieces of fabric 43.5 cm × 90 cm ($17\frac{1}{4}$ in × $35\frac{1}{2}$ in), to attach to the hem of the skirt.
Middle layer: cut five pieces of fabric 41.5 cm × 90 cm ($16\frac{1}{4}$ in × $35\frac{1}{2}$ in), to attach to placement line C.

Top layer: cut three pieces of fabric 38 cm × 90 cm (15 in × 35½ in), to include with the waist seam of the dress.

There is a 1.5 cm (⅝ in) seam and hem allowance.

Fabric quantity
115 cm (45 in) wide: 8.90 m (9¾ yd)

Haberdashery
Thread; 20 cm (8 in) zip, for the skirt, *or* 40 cm (16 in) zip, for the strapless dress; Wundaweb, if required, for the frill hems

Cutting out
2 × back skirt panel and 2 × front skirt panel in fabric or lining. Transfer placement line B from the pattern to the fabric. Cut the frill pieces for the top, middle and bottom layers.

Sewing
1. Join up the ends of the five pieces cut for the bottom layer frill and press. Fold 1.5 cm (⅝ in) onto WS along one edge and press. Fold under the raw edge and stitch by hand or machine, or neaten the raw edge and secure the hem with Wundaweb. Cut the web in half lengthways before inserting it under the edge of the fabric.
2. Divide the other edge of the frill into eight and insert a gathering thread along each section. On the skirt, divide the hem edge into eight. Hold the skirt RS out and slip the frill over it, WS out. Match the eight sections and pin, with the raw edges level. Working on one section at a time, pull up each gathering thread until the frill lies flat on the skirt. Secure the thread ends and even out the gathers. Baste the section. Repeat all round the skirt.
3. With the frill uppermost, machine along the gathering line and through the frill and skirt. Remove the basting, trim the raw edges and neaten.
4. Join up the ends of the top layer pieces, leaving 26 cm (10 in) open in the top of one seam, and press. Fold up a 1.5 cm (⅝ in) hem onto WS, press and finish with stitching or Wundaweb, as described for the bottom layer. At the zip opening, press back the seam allowances.
5. Holding the skirt RS out, slip the upper layer over it, RS out. Pin together, with the frill hip edges 1.5 cm (⅝ in) back from the skirt edge. Insert four gathering threads, one to each skirt section, through both layers.
6. Join the pieces together for the middle layer, and complete the hem edge as for the other layers. Neaten the raw edge, divide it into eight and insert eight gathering threads 1.5 cm (⅝ in) below the neatened edge. At the placement line on the underskirt, divide the skirt into eight. Lift the top layer of the skirt, slide the middle tier over the skirt, both RS out, and arrange so that the gathering line falls over the placement line. Pin at the eight points, pull up the gathering threads and anchor the thread ends; baste. Pull the top layer down and make sure it covers the raw edge. Even out the gathers and baste each section. Stitch the frill to the skirt, making

sure that the stitching falls on top of the gathering line. A small Pattern information and variations

zigzag stitch is useful here.

Remove all basting from the skirt and press. To attach the skirt to the strapless bodice, fold in the zip edges and insert the zip between the skirt edges, holding the frill edges free. Alternatively, for a skirt, fold in the skirt edges and insert the zip, holding the frill free, then attach the waistband.

Drop-waist skirt with overlapping tiers

This is designed to be mid-calf length; for longer or shorter lengths, adjust the length of all pieces.

Cut four gathered skirt panels in lining, as described on page 52, using cutting line A for the drop waist and D for the hem of the lining. There is a 1 cm ($\frac{5}{8}$ in) seam allowance. Using the tier fabric, cut the pieces to be gathered and attached to the lining as follows:

Bottom tier: cut and join five pieces 27.5 cm × 90 cm ($10\frac{3}{4}$ in × 36 in) and attach them to the hem of the lining

Middle tier: cut and join four pieces 24.5 cm × 90 cm ($9\frac{1}{2}$ in × 36 in) and attach them to placement line C

Top tier: cut and join three pieces 18 cm × 90 cm (7 in × 36 in) and attach them to the waist of the lining

There is a 1 cm ($\frac{3}{8}$ in) seam allowance, but if raw edges are left at the lower edges there is no need to cut off the allowance.

Fabric quantities (dress with tiered skirt)
See page 106.

Cutting out and making instructions are also on page 106.

Balloon skirt

This combines the straight skirt and gathered skirt patterns, to be attached to the waist of the strapless bodice or made as a skirt.

Trace the gathered skirt panel to hemline F. For the underskirt, use the straight skirt pattern lengthened by 23 cm (9 in).

There is a 1.5 cm ($\frac{5}{8}$ in) seam allowance throughout.

Fabric quantities (115 cm (45 in) wide)

Size		
12	4.30 m ($4\frac{3}{4}$ yd)
14	4.30 m ($4\frac{3}{4}$ yd)
16	4.80 m ($5\frac{1}{3}$ yd)
18	4.80 m ($5\frac{1}{3}$ yd)
20	4.80 m ($5\frac{1}{3}$ yd)

Haberdashery
Thread

Cutting out
1 × lengthened back skirt, to fold, in lining *or* fabric
1 × lengthened front skirt, to fold, in lining *or* fabric
4 × gathered skirt panels, in fabric

57

Sewing

1. Stitch the darts in the back waist of the underskirt, and press towards the centre. Fold the front waist tucks towards the sides and stitch across the top to anchor them. Stitch the skirt side seams, hold the skirt inside out and leave a 21.5 cm (8$\frac{3}{8}$in) zip opening at the left. Press back the zip edges. Neaten the seams.

2. Stitch and press open all the overskirt seams, leaving 21.5 cm (8$\frac{3}{8}$in) open in the left seam for the zip. Neatening can be omitted. Press back the zip edges. Insert a gathering thread along the edge in each of the four sections at the hem and at the waist edge.

3. Have the underskirt RS out and slide the overskirt over it, WS out, until the hem edges are level. Match the side seams, and pin and match the central overskirt seams to CB and CF of the underskirt. Pull up the hemline gathering threads in each section until the edges lie flat. Even out the gathers and baste. Stitch around the hem on the gathering line. Trim the raw edges and turn the skirt through, bringing the overskirt over the lining until the waist edges are level. Match the side seams and pin. Match the central overskirt seams to CF and CB lining. At the zip opening, have the pressed folds of both layers exactly level and baste them together.

4. Pull up the gathering threads in each section until the overskirt lies flat on the underskirt. Pin and baste through both layers. Machine all round, following the gathering line, to hold securely. Complete by attaching the balloon skirt to the bodice, easing up the gathers more if necessary. Alternatively, attach a waistband.

Straight belt

Cut a rectangle of paper or fabric 13 cm (5$\frac{1}{8}$in) wide and to the length of your waist measurement plus 5.5 cm (2$\frac{1}{8}$in).

A 1.5 cm ($\frac{5}{8}$in) seam allowance is included all round. The fabric is folded, making the finished belt 5 cm (2 in) wide with an overlap to fasten. Cut a piece of pelmet-weight or heavy Vilene 5 cm (2 in) wide and the correct length, or use an alternative belt stiffening.

The width of the pattern can be altered if you wish, although if a straight belt is made wider than about 7 cm (2$\frac{3}{4}$in) it will not be comfortable and will probably wrinkle in wear.

Haberdashery
Thread; belt stiffening 5 cm (2 in) wide; 2 Velcro Spot-Ons *or* 4 cm (1$\frac{1}{2}$in) Velcro *or* 2 hooks and bars

Cutting out
Cut the fabric and stiffening to size, following the paper pattern.

Sewing
1. Fold the fabric lengthways, RS out, and press the fold. Open it out, place the belt stiffening in place with one edge against the fold, and secure. To make Vilene easier to handle, first trim 1.5 cm ($\frac{5}{8}$in) from all edges. Petersham or other stiffening should be the

correct width of the finished belt, but trim 1.5 cm ($\frac{5}{8}$ in) off each
end. If you want the overlap to be pointed or angled, trim it before
stitching.

2. Secure with basting tape or Wundaweb between the two
layers, or by machining all round inside the edge of the stiffening,
or by hand using herringbone stitch over the edge. The choice
depends on how the finished belt is to look. If you plan to add a
beaded design, it is best to stick the layers or hand sew them. If you
intend to add rows of braid, a line of machine stitches would act as
a guide.

3. Fold the edges neatly over the stiffening and baste. Mitre the
fabric at the corners. Press the belt from RS. Fold the unstiffened
piece of fabric over the stiffening, baste along the fold and along
the middle of the belt. Fold in the remaining raw edges and baste.
Press the edges.

4. Complete the belt by slipstitching all the folded edges together
or, if the stiffening was not machined in place, machine all round
the belt once or several times in parallel rows, depending on the
fabric and the finished effect required.

5. Measure the belt round your waist, and mark the amount of
the overlap with a fabric pen. Attach the Velcro by hemming all
round; if you are using a rectangle, first snip off the corners. Sew
the soft side of the Velcro to the upper part of the belt.

6. Attach the hook with buttonhole stitch worked with the
stitches close together. Start by securing the head of the hook
3 mm ($\frac{1}{8}$ in) back from the end of the belt then sew round the loops.
Attach the bar to the belt by stab stitching through each eye and
right through the belt, then work buttonhole stitch as for the
hook. If a metal bar is not available, make a thread loop. Using
thread doubled and run through beeswax to add strength, make a
bar of four or five stitches across the belt, stabbing the needle right
through, then bring the needle to RS and work loop stitch over the
threads on the surface of the fabric. Fasten off all thread strongly
after attaching the fasteners.

Hip sash

Two pieces of fabric 90 cm × 33 cm (36 in × 13 in), joined end to
end, will make a soft tie-sash. Trim the ends at an angle. A 1 cm
($\frac{3}{8}$ in) hem is allowed all round.

Making instructions are on page 76.

Shaped belt

The shaped area at the front of this belt provides a space for
decorative stitching or beading, as well as helping to hold a blouse
in position. The belt fastens at CB.

Cut a rectangle of paper to 13 cm ($5\frac{1}{8}$ in) width and length as
follows:

Size	12	75.5 cm ($29\frac{3}{4}$ in)	18	87.5 cm ($34\frac{1}{2}$ in)
	14	78.5 cm ($30\frac{3}{4}$ in)	20	92.5 cm ($36\frac{1}{4}$ in)
	16	84 cm (33 in)		

Note: if you plan to fasten the belt with Velcro, lengthen the paper by 5 cm (2 in) before shaping.

Fold the paper in half across the length. Mark the fold CF. Draw the shape of the belt illustrated, making it 6 cm (2$\frac{3}{8}$ in) wide where it fastens at CB. This pattern will be cut twice to a fold in fabric and once in pelmet-weight or heavy Vilene, omitting the seam allowance to reduce bulk.

1.5 cm ($\frac{5}{8}$ in) seam allowances and a 2.5 cm (1 in) overlap are included.

The same shape can be used as a waistband but with the fastening at the left, see below.

Haberdashery
Thread; Vilene; 3–4 cm (1$\frac{1}{4}$–1$\frac{1}{2}$ in) Velcro

Cutting out
2 × fabric, to length plus overlap
1 × medium or soft Vilene, cut to shape

For quilting or embroidery, mark the shape of the belt, attach backing or wadding, and work the decoration. Re-measure the belt and cut out.

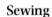

Sewing
1. Baste the Vilene to WS one piece of fabric. Place the second piece of fabric against it, with the fabric RS together, and baste. With the Vilene uppermost, stitch all round 1 cm ($\frac{3}{8}$ in) inside the edge, making a neat point and corners. Leave a gap in the stitching in the lower straight edge 10 cm (4 in) long.
2. Remove the basting. Press the stitching, and trim and snip the raw edges all round except along the gap. Fold each seam allowance beside the gap WS down onto WS belt, and press so that the raw edges meet.
3. Turn the belt RS out and push into the corners, using a bodkin. Roll all the edges, baste and press. Slipstitch the folds together along the gap. Remove the basting.
4. Attach the Velcro to the overlap, placing the soft side on the outer part and snipping off the corners. Hem all round or use a small zigzag machine stitch.

Shaped waistband

To make the pattern, cut the rectangle to size in paper:

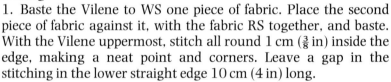

Size		
12	75.5 cm × 13 cm	(29$\frac{3}{4}$ in × 5$\frac{1}{8}$ in)
14	78.5 cm × 13 cm	(30$\frac{7}{8}$ in × 5$\frac{1}{8}$ in)
16	84 cm × 13 cm	(33 in × 5$\frac{1}{8}$ in)
18	87.5 cm × 13 cm	(34$\frac{3}{8}$ in × 5$\frac{1}{8}$ in)
20	92.5 cm × 13 cm	(36$\frac{3}{8}$ in × 5$\frac{1}{8}$ in)

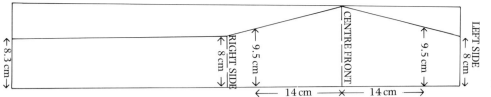

SHAPED WAISTBAND

Mark CF, measuring from the *left* side:

Size		
12	20.5 cm	(8 in)
14	21.7 cm	($8\frac{1}{2}$ in)
16	23 cm	(9 in)
18	24.2 cm	($9\frac{1}{2}$ in)
20	25.8 cm	($10\frac{1}{8}$ in)

Mark to the *right* of CF:

Size		
12	19 cm	($7\frac{1}{2}$ in)
14	20.2 cm	(8 in)
16	21.5 cm	($8\frac{3}{8}$ in)
18	22.7 cm	($8\frac{7}{8}$ in)
20	24.3 cm	($9\frac{1}{2}$ in)

Draw cutting lines to join all points.

Use the pattern right side up on the fabric.

Cutting out

2 × waistband; 1 × heavy Vilene

Making instructions are on page 81.

Pleated belt

This is a wide cummerbund of pleated fabric.

Fabric quantity

115 cm (45 in) wide: 50 cm ($\frac{1}{2}$ yd)

Haberdashery

Thread; 50 cm (20 in) heavy Vilene *or* 20 cm ($\frac{1}{4}$ yd) light Vilene; 9 cm ($3\frac{1}{2}$ in) hook-and-eye tape *or* 6–8 hooks and bars; 5–6 m ($5\frac{1}{2}$–$6\frac{1}{2}$ yd) narrow picot edge satin ribbon, to match or contrast with the fabric (optional).

Cutting out

1 × fabric 39 cm ($15\frac{1}{4}$ in) wide × waist measurement plus 5.5 cm ($2\frac{1}{4}$ in)

1 × pelmet-weight or heavy Vilene 9 cm ($3\frac{1}{2}$ in) wide × fabric length minus 3 cm ($1\frac{1}{4}$ in)

These measurements allow for an overlap of 2.5 cm (1 in); if you plan to fasten the belt with Velcro, cut the fabric 5 cm (2 in) longer.

Sewing

1. Make 1.5 cm ($\frac{5}{8}$ in) parallel tucks along half the fabric as follows:

Fold the fabric RS out along the middle and press. Using a fabric pen, mark a few dots at one end 1.5 cm ($\frac{5}{8}$ in) from the fold. Machine at this distance from the fold, allowing the fold to follow the appropriate groove in the needle plate.

Press the stitching smooth. Measure from the stitching 3 cm ($1\frac{1}{4}$ in) in both directions, fold, press and stitch two more tucks, then make two more in the same way. The tucks could be less wide, in which case make more. Check the size by folding in the remaining pieces of fabric to make sure that the edges can be joined. Press all the tucks to lie downwards.

2. Attach the ribbon, placing it on top or just under the edge of each tuck, and stitch.

3. Place the Vilene on WS, to cover the tucks. Attach with herringbone stitch along the edges and machine across the ends.

4. Fold the belt WS out, match the long raw edges and stitch, leaving a 12 cm (5 in) gap in the middle. Press the raw edges flat to one side and with the seam along the middle of the belt. Stitch across the ends, trim and turn the belt RS out. Push out the corners with a bodkin. Slipstitch the gap in the back of the belt.

5. Try on and mark the overlap. Stitch the hook tape in position, with the hook part 1.5 cm ($\frac{5}{8}$ in) back from the edge to conceal the fasteners. Machine in place, taking care to stitch along the edges of the tape and not to break the machine needle. Alternatively, attach separate hooks and bars spaced across the belt, using buttonhole stitch for strength and neatness.

Back bow

A big stiffened bow with long tails, this is to attach to the back waist of a skirt or waisted dress. The tail measurements given are for an ankle-length skirt. For a shorter skirt, reduce the measurements.

A 1.5 cm ($\frac{5}{8}$ in) seam allowance is included.

Fabric quantity
115 cm (45 in) wide: 80 cm ($\frac{7}{8}$ yd)

Haberdashery
Thread; 80 cm ($\frac{7}{8}$ yd) light sew-in or iron-on Vilene

Cutting out
Bow: 1 × fabric 68 cm × 40 cm ($26\frac{3}{4}$ in × $15\frac{3}{4}$ in); 1 × Vilene same size
Centre strip: 1 × fabric 10 cm × 8 cm (4 in × $3\frac{1}{8}$ in); 1 × Vilene same size
Tails: 1 × fabric 73 cm × 25 cm ($28\frac{3}{4}$ in × $9\frac{3}{4}$ in); 1 × Vilene same size

Sewing
1. Press or baste the Vilene to WS bow. Fold the fabric RS together and stitch the long edges together. Turn RS out. Do not press but fold with the seam 5 cm (2 in) above the lower fold.

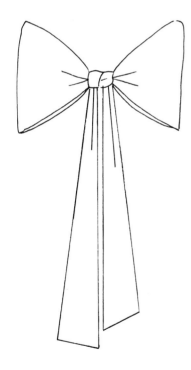

2. Fold the strip RS together and stitch the long edges together. Turn RS out and press.

3. Fold the bow over to WS to overlap by 2 cm ($\frac{3}{4}$ in) at the centre. Gather across the centre through all thicknesses. Wrap the strip round the centre of the bow, overlap the ends and stitch together.

4. To make the tail, press or baste the Vilene to WS fabric. Fold the tail lengthways, RS together, and pin. Trim each end at 45 degrees. Stitch the ends and the long side, leaving a 8–10 cm ($3\frac{1}{4}$–4 in) gap for turning through. Press the stitching and press the seam allowances onto WS fabric beside the gap. Trim and snip the remaining raw edges.

5. Turn the tail RS out. Push out the points with a bodkin, roll the edges and press. Slipstitch along the gap.

6. Fold the tail over 30 cm (12 in) from one end. Fold a deep pleat across the width of the tail and sew firmly to the back of the bow.

7. The bow can be sewn to the pleated belt or you can make it detachable by using two Velcro Spot-Ons; sew the soft side under the edge of the top and bottom tucks of the belt.

Off-shoulder frill

A wide frill, this is pulled up to size with elastic, to attach to the strapless bodice, ruched bodice or camisole. The frill is 3 m ($3\frac{1}{4}$ yd) long and 20 cm (8 in) wide. Make joins in the fabric if necessary.

   No hem allowance is included on the long edges.

Fabric quantity
115 cm (45 in) wide: 60 cm ($\frac{2}{3}$ yd)

Haberdashery
Thread; 3 m ($3\frac{1}{4}$ yd) narrow elastic plus 3 m ($3\frac{1}{4}$ yd) bought bias binding *or* shirring elastic

Cutting out
Pieces of fabric to total 3 m ($3\frac{1}{4}$ yd) in length. Use pinking shears on non-fraying fabrics such as taffeta and net for an unstitched edge.

Sewing
1. Join the pieces end to end with a hairline seam and press.

2. If the edges are not to be left raw, work a very small zigzag over the raw edge. Alternatively, use a scallop machine embroidery pattern, carefully trimming off the surplus fabric; stitch 3 mm ($\frac{1}{8}$ in) wide satin ribbon over the raw edge; or fold under the raw edge by a minimum amount and zigzag over it with a small stitch. This last technique is suitable for fine, fraying fabrics such as voile and chiffon, and also jersey which can be pulled while stitching to produce a fluted edge.

3. On WS, 7 cm ($2\frac{3}{4}$ in) from the upper edge, apply the bias binding flat and stitch along each edge. Turn under the ends to meet each other, level with one of the seams in the frill. Thread the elastic through the binding, pull it up to size and join the ends.

Alternatively, work four or five rows of shirring, more if necessary, following the instructions on page 68.

Frilly sleeve

A double frill, pulled up with elastic, this can be attached to either the strapless bodice or the ruched bodice.

There is no hem allowance on the outer edge. 2 cm ($\frac{3}{4}$ in) is allowed for the elastic casing.

Fabric quantity
115 cm (45 in): 30 cm ($\frac{1}{3}$ yd)

Haberdashery
Thread; narrow elastic

Cutting out
(For each sleeve)
Under frill fabric: 80 cm × 18 cm (32 in × 7 in)
Upper frill fabric: 80 cm × 12 cm (32 in × $4\frac{3}{4}$ in)

If the frill edges are to be left unhemmed, the fabric could be cut with pinking shears.

Sewing
1. Fold each frill RS together and join across the short end.
2. Finish the outer edges of the frills with zigzag or narrow hem if required.
3. With WS frills towards you, slip the narrow frill over the wide one, with the raw edge of the wide frill 5 mm ($\frac{1}{4}$ in) within that of the narrow frill. Turn a 2 cm ($\frac{3}{4}$ in) hem onto the inside, folding the edge that extends over onto the other edge. Stitch the hem, leaving a gap for threading the elastic.
4. Insert the elastic and pull up tightly if the sleeve is to be worn separately. Have the sleeve looser if you propose to attach it to the dress at the underarm. Slipstitch the edge of the sleeve to the finished edge of the armhole.

Alternatively, attach the sleeve at two points only with bar tacks.

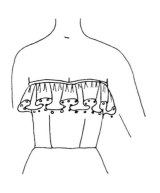

Flat bodice frill

Here the fabric is used double, gathered, to attach to the upper edge of the strapless bodice.

A 1 cm ($\frac{3}{8}$ in) seam allowance is included.

Fabric quantity
115 cm (45 in): 30 cm ($\frac{1}{3}$ yd)

Haberdashery
Thread; pearls or beads (optional)

Cutting out

$2 \times$ fabric $90\,\text{cm} \times 16\,\text{cm}$ ($36\,\text{in} \times 6\frac{1}{4}\,\text{in}$)

$1 \times 2.5\,\text{cm}$ ($1\,\text{in}$) bias strip $\times$ the following length:

Size		
12	$91\,\text{cm}$	($35\frac{3}{4}\,\text{in}$)
14	$93\,\text{cm}$	($36\frac{1}{2}\,\text{in}$)
16	$96\,\text{cm}$	($37\frac{3}{4}\,\text{in}$)
18	$101\,\text{cm}$	($39\frac{3}{4}\,\text{in}$)
20	$104\,\text{cm}$	($41\,\text{in}$)

Sewing

1. Join the two pieces of fabric across one short end. Fold the frill RS together, stitch across the short ends and trim. Turn the frill RS out and press.

2. Insert a gathering thread along the frill through the raw edges. Divide the frill into four and mark. Divide the upper edge of bodice into four. Place the frill RS up on RS bodice, match the quarters and pin, matching the finished ends to the zip edges of the bodice. Pull up the gathering threads, even out the gathers and baste the frill to the bodice.

3. Cut off $1.5\,\text{cm}$ ($\frac{5}{8}\,\text{in}$) seam allowance from the upper edge of the bodice before applying the binding.

4. Join the bias strips if necessary. Pass the binding through a tape maker and press. Open out one fold, place the binding RS down on WS bodice, with the edges level, and baste. Fold in the ends of the binding and fold the remaining edge of the binding onto RS bodice. Baste and stitch in place along the edge of the binding. Decorate the edge of the frill if desired.

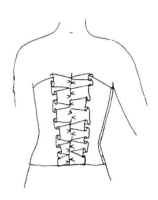

Centre front frill

A shaped rectangle of fabric gathered and attached to the CF seam of the strapless bodice with a gathered panel or the ruched bodice.

To make the pattern, rule a line $48\,\text{cm}$ ($19\,\text{in}$) long and mark it 'CF'. Rule a line at each end at 90 degrees, to the following lengths:

Upper edge:

Size		
12	$12\,\text{cm}$	($4\frac{3}{4}\,\text{in}$)
14	$12.5\,\text{cm}$	($5\,\text{in}$)
16	$13.5\,\text{cm}$	($5\frac{3}{8}\,\text{in}$)
18	$14\,\text{cm}$	($5\frac{1}{2}\,\text{in}$)
20	$14.5\,\text{cm}$	($5\frac{3}{4}\,\text{in}$)

Lower edge:

Size		
12	$10.5\,\text{cm}$	($4\frac{1}{8}\,\text{in}$)
14	$11\,\text{cm}$	($4\frac{3}{8}\,\text{in}$)
16	$11.5\,\text{cm}$	($4\frac{1}{2}\,\text{in}$)
18	$12\,\text{cm}$	($4\frac{3}{4}\,\text{in}$)
20	$12.5\,\text{cm}$	($5\,\text{in}$)

Label the first line 'Fold' and mark SG parallel wih it. Rule final line. Cut this pattern to the fold of the fabric.

There is a $1.5\,\text{cm}$ ($\frac{5}{8}\,\text{in}$) seam allowance.

Making instructions are on page 77.

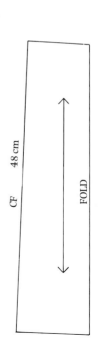

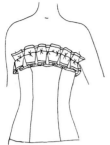

Pleated bodice frill

A single piece of fabric is box-pleated and applied flat to the upper edge of the strapless bodice.

You will need a piece of fabric, joined where necessary, 4 cm ($1\frac{5}{8}$ in) wide and cut to the following length:

Size	
12	2.97 m (3 yd 9 in)
14	3.12 m (3 yd 14 in)
16	3.27 m (3 yd 20 in)
18	3.49 m (3 yd 26 in)
20	3.64 m (3 yd 32 in)

There is no seam allowance on the long edges. There is an allowance for slight gathering along the centre of the frill after pleating.

Making instructions are on page 110.

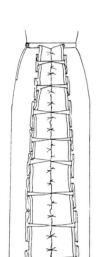

Pleated frill for skirt

This wide, box-pleated frill can be attached to CB of the ankle-length skirt. If you are making it for a short skirt, adjust the length. If a long skirt is not made to the pattern length, the frill will need adjusting.

Draw a line 2.65 m (2 yd $31\frac{1}{2}$ in) long. Mark it 'CB Fold'. Rule lines at right angles, 11 cm ($4\frac{1}{4}$ in) long at the top, and 24 cm ($9\frac{1}{2}$ in) long at the base. Complete the pattern shape.

Cut one piece to the fold and open out. There is no seam allowance on the long edge; 1 cm ($\frac{3}{8}$ in) is allowed at top and bottom. There is an allowance for slight gathering along CB after pleating.

Making instructions are on page 110.

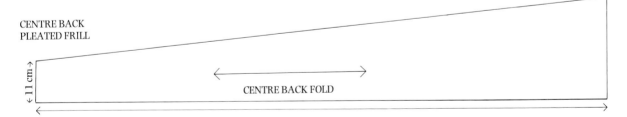

CENTRE BACK
PLEATED FRILL

← 11 cm →

CENTRE BACK FOLD

Sculptured strap

A single strap with a shaped end, this can be attached to a plain, strapless bodice. Alternatively, attach it to the camisole, in which case two straps will be needed. The shaped end extends over the bodice edge and provides an area for beading or decorative stitching. Select a leaf or diamond shape, shown full size below for you to trace.

Cut two pieces of fabric, shaped and to the measurements given on the illustration. A 1.5 cm ($\frac{5}{8}$ in) seam has been allowed. Cut one piece of light iron-on Vilene the same shape. Attach the Vilene to WS of one strap. Mark your chosen shape on the Vilene, using a fabric pen.

Making instructions are on page 96.

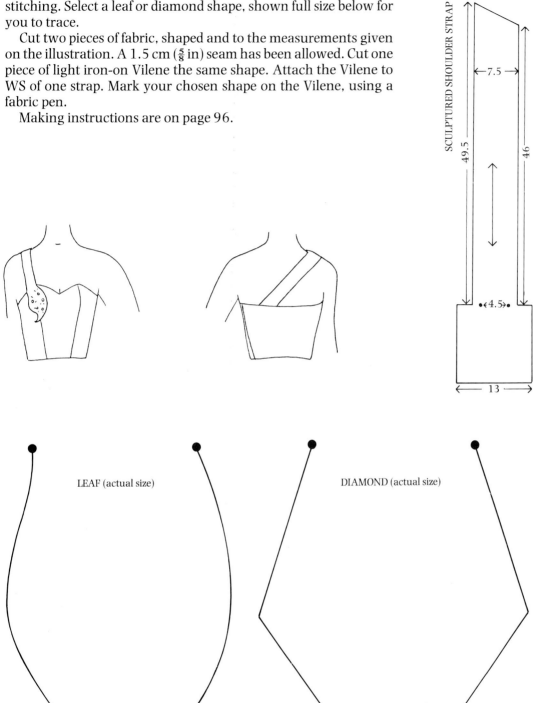

SCULPTURED SHOULDER STRAP

49.5   7.5   46   4.5   13   13

LEAF (actual size)

DIAMOND (actual size)

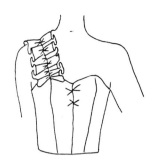

Elasticated shoulder strap

A single piece of fabric makes one wide shoulder strap, to attach to the strapless bodice. It is gathered to size and held in place with elastic stitched along the middle.

Fabric quantity
75 cm × 19 cm (29½ in × 7½ in)
 A 1 cm (⅜ in) hem is allowed.

Haberdashery
Thread; shirring elastic

Cutting out
1 or 2 straps to size above

Sewing
1. Fold the fabric RS together, stitch the long edges and turn RS out. Press with the seam along the middle.
2. Wind the shirring elastic onto a spool exactly as you do when winding thread, except that the elastic must not pass through the needle. If you have a machine that only winds thread via the needle, you will have to wind the elastic by hand although the result will be much less satisfactory.
3. Thread the machine with the spool of elastic and sewing thread on the top; set it to a long straight stitch. With the fabric RS up, stitch along the centre then make further rows each side, the width of the machine foot apart. Flatten the fabric as you sew; the more rows you work, the more gathered it becomes. Work alternately in each direction to prevent any drag one way. Using a small stitch and thread top and bottom, sew across the strap ends several times to prevent the threads coming out.
 If the strap is not being inserted in the upper edge of the bodice between the bodice and the lining, neaten the raw edges with a bias strip to further prevent the threads coming loose.
4. Hold the strap in the vapour from boiling water, to shrink the elastic to its former state and make a tighter strap.
 An alternative method of using shirring elastic is to lay it in lines on WS fabric, stretching it as you zigzag over it.

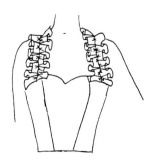

Elasticated halter strap

A single piece of fabric gathered along the centre forms a halter to attach to the strapless bodice.

Fabric quantity
Two pieces of fabric 54 cm × 19 cm (21¼ in × 7½ in)
 A 1 cm (⅜ in) hem is allowed on each edge.

Cape wrap

This one-size, softly draped cover-up can be worn over any of the dresses or tops. The wrists are pulled in with elastic.

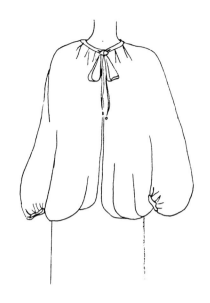

Fabric quantity
115 cm (45 in): 1.30 m (1⅜ yd)

Haberdashery
Thread; narrow web elastic for wrists; 2 silver beads or filigree buttons (optional)

Cutting out
Fold the fabric lengthways and cut the oval shape shown. On the centre fold, scoop out a neckline shape 15 cm (6 in) wide and 2 cm (¾ in) deep at the middle. Cut through one layer only from the base of the neckline to the opposite side of the fabric. Curve the two corners of this layer.

Cut bias strips 2.5 cm (1 in) wide from surplus fabric and join to make a strip 115 cm (45 in) long, for the neckline.

Making instructions are on page 82.

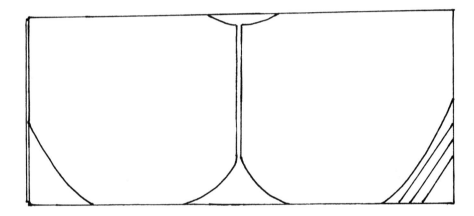

Clutch bag

This small bag has gussets stiffened with Vilene. It provides a base for decorative features, beading etc. Decoration should be worked before cutting out, with the exception of beads.

Make the pattern as shown from a piece of paper 53 cm × 29 cm

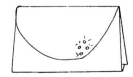

Pattern information and variations   (21 in × 11½ in). Select the flap shape and mark it. Mark the other fold lines. Cut the gusset pattern 17 cm × 5 cm (6¾ in × 2 in).
There is a 1 cm (⅜ in) seam allowance all round.

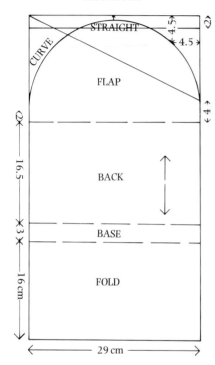

CLUTCH BAG

Fabric quantity
60 cm (23½ in) in fabric
60 cm (23½ in) in lining *or* fabric
60 cm (23½ in) heavy Vilene
20 cm (8 in) medium-weight iron-on Vilene

Cutting out
1 bag piece in fabric
1 bag piece in lining *or* fabric
1 bag piece in pelmet-weight or heavy Vilene
1 bag piece in thin wadding
2 gussets in fabric
2 gussets in fabric *or* lining
2 gussets in medium-weight iron-on Vilene
Trim the seam allowance from the heavy Vilene and score along the foldlines.

Haberdashery
Thread; 1 or 2 Velcro Spot-Ons to fasten

Sewing
1. With the bag fabric WS up, baste the wadding in place, put the heavy Vilene on top and remove any wadding extending beyond the Vilene.
2. On the bag and the lining, snip the edge of the fabric 1 cm (⅜ in) where the gusset fits. Press the medium-weight Vilene to WS gussets and place them RS down on RS bag, matching the raw edges between snips. Stitch the gusset ends. Swivel the bag until the raw edges are level with the gusset sides then stitch from the base to the upper edge of the bag. Turn the bag RS out.
3. Turn all the raw edges over the edge of the Vilene to the inside and baste, with the exception of the edge opposite the flap.
4. Attach the gussets to the lining in the same way. Place the end of the lining to the bag, RS together and matching the edges at the end opposite the flap. Stitch across. Fold the lining over the edge and push inside the bag.
5. Keeping the lining smooth, fold in all the raw edges and baste, with the edge of the lining 3 mm (⅛ in) inside the edge of the bag. Hem in place.
You can attach a length of cord, filled rouleau, plait or chain if you want a handle or shoulder strap on the bag.
6. Attach the Velcro Spot-Ons to the flap, hemming round each part.

4 The Outfits

I have combined pattern pieces in different ways to produce the outfits shown in the photographs. They show a variety of shapes, styles and fabrics and different decorative techniques. You can select from those shown, or you can make up your own variations.

STRAPLESS DRESS

Here is a classic dress that is always in fashion. The bodice is strapless and boned, and the skirt is a full circle to mid-calf or ankle length. It is shown made in crisp silk in vivid turquoise, with one extravagant shoulder strap of full-blown red roses; a spray of smaller roses could decorate the flap of a bag (see page 118 for instructions).

The bodice is self-lined, with the zip inserted in the left side seam. The alternative gathered panel has been used at CF, and the waist seam is piped. The roses are made from varying widths of satin ribbon, attached to a fabric strap. Any on a bag would be attached directly to the fabric.

Fabric
102 cm (40 in) wide silk
All sizes, dress and bag:
mid-calf length   6.10 m ($6\frac{2}{3}$ yd)
ankle length   5.40 m ($5\frac{7}{8}$ yd)

Haberdashery
Thread: 2 reels
Zip: 40 cm (16 in)
Rigilene boning: 80 cm (31 in)
Piping cord: waist length
Hook and eye: 1
Light Fold-a-Band: 70 cm (28 in), for the strap
Ribbon: sufficient to make five large roses of three layers, (and three small roses of three layers for a bag), all with double centres of narrow ribbon (see page 118)
Double satin, 75 mm (3 in) wide: 2.60 m ($2\frac{7}{8}$ yd)
Double satin, 50 mm (2 in) wide: 3 m ($3\frac{1}{4}$ yd)
Jacquard ribbon, 40 mm ($1\frac{5}{8}$ in) wide: 2.20 m ($2\frac{1}{2}$ yd)
Picot edge ribbon, 10 mm ($\frac{3}{8}$ in) wide: 4 m ($4\frac{1}{3}$ yd)
Double satin, 3 mm ($\frac{1}{8}$ in) wide: 4 m ($4\frac{1}{3}$ yd)

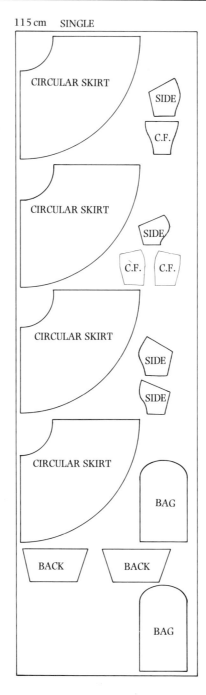

115 cm   SINGLE

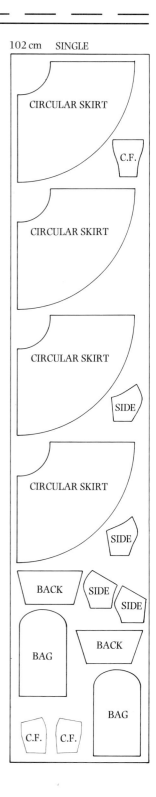

102 cm   SINGLE

72

Cutting out

Bodice (full-size pattern):
2 × gathered CF panel
1 × plain CF panel
4 × side front
2 × back bodice, to fold
1 × 2.5 cm (1 in) bias strip × waist size plus 3 cm (1¼ in), for the piping
1 × 9 cm (3½ in) × 70 cm (28 in) straight piece, for the strap
1 × 2.5 cm (1 in) bias strip × 90 cm (36 in), for the boning

Skirt (measurement pattern, page 50):
4 quarter circles, to D or 2 half circles and omit CF and CB seams.

Sewing

BODICE

1. *Seams.* Gather between the dots in CF panel pieces and pull up to 6 cm (2⅜ in). With RS together, stitch and press the CF seam. Join the side front panels to the centre section along the curved seams, stitch and press. Attach the back bodice to the front along the right side seam only.

2. *Lining.* Join the side and front panels to the plain CF panel along the curved seams. Press. Join the back bodice to the front, holding it with the raw edges facing away from the body. Stitch and press the right side seam only. Using the long bias strip, place it on WS lining, centre the strip over the seam and stitch a channel for the boning. Sew two parallel rows 1.5 cm (⅝ in) apart. Stitch two more channels, one over the side seam and the other 2 cm (1¼ in) inside the raw edge on the back.

3. *Upper edge.* With the bodice and bodice lining RS together, match CF, curved seams and side seam. Stitch along the upper edge, catching in the ends of the bias strip. Trim and press flat. Stitch again through the lining and seam allowances 2 mm ($\frac{1}{16}$ in)

inside the upper edge of the bodice.

4. *Boning.* Insert the Rigilene boning in the channels, trimming the ends 2 cm ($\frac{3}{4}$ in) above the waist edge. Pin across the channels at the waist.

5. *Variations.* If a plain front panel is used, cut the pattern once to the fold, the same as for the lining. If you plan to attach two shoulder straps or a halter strap, the boning on the curved front seams can be omitted. If you prefer a back zip, cut the back bodice pattern with a seam, placing the edge of the pattern 1.5 cm ($\frac{5}{8}$ in) from the edge of the fabric. Make a corresponding seam in the skirt.

SKIRT

1. *Seams.* With the fabric RS together, stitch, neaten and press open the seams at CB, CF and the right side. At the left seam, stitch to within 20 cm (8 in) of the waist edge.

2. *Piping.* Wrap the bias fabric around the cord, RS out, and stitch beside the cord from end to end. Place on RS bodice waist with all raw edges level. Stitch the piping to the bodice.

3. *Waist seam.* If you are using the lower waistline, gather each panel. Hold the skirt WS out and put the bodice inside so RS are together. Match the seams and zip edges. Baste around the waist through all layers, including the piping seam allowances. Stitch the waistline from the bodice side, carefully following the piping stitching. Trim the edges and neaten.

4. *Variations.* If the skirt is cut in two half circles, there will be two side seams only to stitch. If the fabric is too narrow to cut a full-length skirt, join on the additional fabric necessary and complete cutting the hemline before stitching the seams. For a gathered skirt, cut a lower waist and hemline.

5. *Zip.* Hold the bodice lining clear of the zip edges and fold under 1 cm ($\frac{3}{8}$ in) along the back edge of the bodice and into the skirt seam. Press. Note that the fold does not meet the seam at the back of the zip opening. This is so that the zip will be covered when fastened.

With the zip closed, place the tape under the pressed edge, with the fold close to the teeth and the slider 1 cm ($\frac{3}{8}$ in) below the seam at the upper edge of the bodice. Baste in place and stitch by hand or machine close to the edge of the fabric.

On the front edge of the bodice, fold back and press 1.5 cm ($\frac{5}{8}$ in). Overlap this edge onto the zip so that the fold rests on the stitching. Match the waist seam and upper edge seam and secure with basting tape. Baste and stitch the second side of the zip by hand, or machine beside the teeth. Stop at the bottom and fasten off securely; do not stitch across the base of the zip or a pucker will form.

On the inside, bring the lining onto the bodice, matching the seams. Baste in place above the waistline. With the raw edges of the waist seam facing the bodice, fold under the raw edge of the bodice along the waist and beside the zip. Baste and hem to finish. Attach the hook and eye at the upper edge of the bodice.

6. *Hem.* Allow the dress to hang for a few days; the skirt will drop. Mark the hemlines level, measuring an even distance from the floor. If you have someone to help you, stand at the top of the stairs and the helper can sit comfortably on the step below.

Trim the hem, leaving sufficient to turn up a narrow hem all round. Machine. Press the dress and hang up.

7. *Strap.* Press the Fold-a-Band to WS fabric. Cut around the outer edge, leaving a seam allowance. Fold RS together along the perforations, stitch across one end and along the side so that the stitches are off the Fold-a-Band. Press the stitching, trim the corners and turn the strap RS out, using a knitting needle or bodkin to push against the stitched end. Roll the seam to the edge and press the strap.

Pin the strap with the finished end inside the upper edge of the bodice, level with the front seam. Pin the other end inside the back bodice on the left. Try on the dress and adjust the length. Stitch the strap firmly to the bodice lining, trimming off the surplus and oversewing the raw edges neatly.

8. *Roses.* Make ribbon roses as described on page 118, finishing with 4 cm ($1\frac{1}{2}$ in) loops of picot edge ribbon and 3 mm ($\frac{1}{8}$ in) ribbon to make centres. Space out five roses along the strap and sew in place.

DRESS WITH SASH

An easy-fit elegant dress with scoop neck and extended shoulder, this can be worn straight or lifted at the hips with a wide tie sash.

Made here in a beautiful black and white silk Jacquard fabric, the dress suits classic accessories. The neckline may be hemmed or bound; the skirt has a side slit.

Fabric
115 cm (45 in) wide silk Jacquard
Dress and sash:

Size	12	3.80 m ($4\frac{1}{3}$ yd)
	14	3.80 m ($4\frac{1}{3}$ yd)
	16	3.80 m ($4\frac{1}{3}$ yd)
	18	3.90 m ($4\frac{1}{3}$ yd)
	20	3.90 m ($4\frac{1}{3}$ yd)

Haberdashery
Thread: 2 reels

Cutting out
Cap-sleeve pattern (full-size), lengthened as described on page 36:
2 × back/front, to fold, round neck
1 × 2.5 cm (1 in) bias strip for the neckline, to length given on page 36
2 × sash pattern (see page 59)

Sewing
1. *Side seams.* With the dress back and front RS together, baste the side seams from the sleeve edge to the hem. Baste the shoulders and try on. Adjust the side seams and widen the neckline if necessary. Stitch the side seams, but on the left seam stop the stitching and fasten off 30 cm ($11\frac{3}{4}$ in) above the hem edge, for a side slit. Remove the basting in the seam but not the slit. Press the seams open and neaten the edges, including the slit.

2. *Shoulders.* Baste and stitch the shoulder seams. Press open and neaten. Fold a narrow hem onto WS around the armhole, baste and slip hem or machine all round. At the underarm, snip the seam allowances twice to allow the seam to lie flat. Overcast the raw edges.

3. *Neck edge.* To finish with a hem, trim 5 mm ($\frac{1}{4}$ in) from the front neck in a gentle curve then baste a hem to match the armhole, first across the front neck and then across the back. Press and stitch all round the neck edge with RS uppermost. Machine a neat V of stitching at the shoulders.

To bind the neckline, trim 1 cm ($\frac{3}{8}$ in) from the back neck edge and on the front at the shoulders, curving gently to take off 2 cm ($\frac{3}{4}$ in) at CF.

Pass the bias strip through a tape maker, press and apply the binding RS down to RS neckline. Beginning at CB and leaving an end for joining, open out one fold of the binding and baste in position, taking 5 mm ($\frac{1}{4}$ in) seam allowance. At the shoulders, snip the seam allowance to produce an edge on which to put the binding. At CB, make a neat join on SG as follows. Open out the binding, fold back one end and press. Fold back the other end to meet it and press. The easiest way to make the join is to slipstitch the folds together by hand, but if you prefer you can lift up the ends and machine along the crease. The fabric is on the cross at this point so take care not to stretch it. If it is stitched by machine, it will need repressing. Trim the raw edges. Stitch all round the neck to attach the binding. Remove the basting, trim the raw edges and roll the binding to WS dress. Bring the folded edge onto the stitching and baste. Finish by hemming along the edge of the binding by hand; alternatively, work a decorative

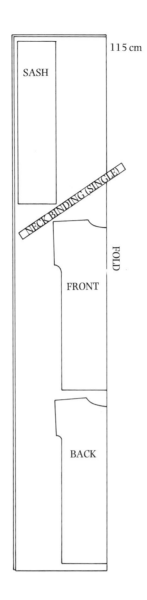

machine stitch round the neck from RS.

4. *Sash.* With the pieces RS together, join the short straight ends. This seam may be visible in wear so make a welt, French or hairline seam, depending on the type of fabric. Turn a narrow hem and baste all round the sash; mitre the corners carefully, hemming them by hand. Press, then machine the hem.

Alternatively, make a narrow double sash. Follow the measurements given on page 59 but do not shape the ends. Join the two pieces as described for a single sash. Fold the sash WS out with the edges level, and stitch across the ends and along the side. Shape the ends if you wish. Leave a 10 cm (4 in) gap in the stitching. Press the line of stitching, trim the raw edges and cut off the corners. Press back the seam allowance on both sides of the gap. Turn the sash RS out, using a rouleau needle to push against the ends. Roll the seam to the edge, push out the corners with the point of a bodkin and press. Slipstitch the gap.

5. *Hem and side slit.* Try on the dress, tie the sash and mark the hemline. At the slit, open out the seam allowances and fold up the hem onto WS. Baste along the hem fold. Check the comparative length of the side seams, especially if using soft or floppy fabric. Press the lower edge. Complete the hem, making it as deep as the fabric will allow. Either neaten the raw edge and catch stitch or, on fine fabrics, fold the raw edge under and slip hem. Fold the side slit over the hem and catch down with loop stitch worked neatly over the edge. Hold back the seam allowance of the side slit with catch stitch or, with firm fabrics, a narrow strip of Wundaweb placed between the seam allowance and the dress. At the top of the slit, work a bar tack on WS.

6. *Hat band.* Make as for the single or double sash. Measure round the hat and cut the band to a suitable width. Leave tie ends.

DROP-WAIST STRAPLESS DRESS

This pretty dress has a self-lined bodice with a centre frill and gathered skirt. It is made in a lovely pink and cream striped slub silk.

The instructions show the skirt cut in the conventional way, with a lengthways grain running from waist to hem; the fabric shown in the photograph was turned round so that the stripes run vertically.

For this dress, the strapless bodice pattern has been lengthened, and four panels of gathered skirt attached.

Fabric
90 cm (36 in) wide slub silk
All sizes: 4.80 m (5⅓ yd)

Haberdashery
Thread: 2 reels
Zip: 40 cm (16 in)
Rigilene boning: 127 cm (50 in)
Grosgrain ribbon: waist length plus 5 cm (2 in), for the waistline stay
Hooks and eyes: 2 small

Cutting out
Strapless bodice (full-size pattern), lengthened as described on page 33:
2 × back, to fold
4 × side front
2 × CF, to fold or two whole panels
1 × 2.5 cm (1 in) bias strip × 1.40 m (1⅔ yd), for the boning
1 × CF frill (diagram pattern), to fold
4 × gathered skirt panels, to hemline E and waistline A
    Mark CF, CB of the bodice.

Sewing
1. *Frill.* Fold a narrow hem along the short edges and stitch. Make matching hems on both long edges. Fold and press. Insert a

gathering thread along the central crease, securing the thread at one end.

2. *Bodice.* Make up the bodice and lining and insert the Rigilene boning as described under instructions on page 74.

3. *Attaching the frill.* Place the frill RS up on RS bodice, matching the gathering thread to CF. Pin at the upper edge of the bodice and 2 cm ($\frac{3}{4}$ in) above the waist edge. Pull up the gathers and even out, then baste and stitch to the bodice with a small zigzag stitch worked down the middle of the frill. Stitch the frill to the bodice only, not through the lining.

4. *Skirt.* With RS together, stitch, press and neaten all four seams, leaving one of them open for 15.5 cm (6 in) below the waist. Insert a gathering thread along the waist edge of each panel.

5. *Waist join.* With bodice RS out and skirt WS out, slip the skirt over the bodice and match the raw edges. Match the bodice side seams and CB and CF to the skirt seams. Pin and pull up the gathering threads to fit. Anchor the thread ends, even out the gathers in each section and baste round the waist. Stitch the bodice to the skirt, sewing with the gathers uppermost and keeping the bodice lining clear. Trim and neaten the seam allowances.

6. *Zip.* Snip the bodice and lining seam allowances at the waist to enable them to be pressed flat, then follow instruction 5 on page 74 for inserting the zip.

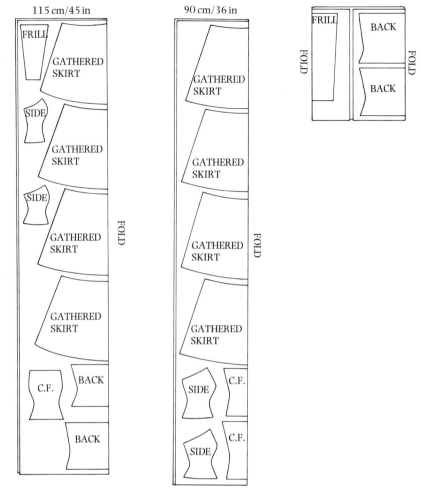

STRAPLESS DRESS WITH FRILL

7. *Waistline stay and frill.* Make the waistline stay, attaching the hooks and eyes to the ends. Sew to the bodice lining with several bar tacks. On RS the corners of the frill may need to be attached to the bodice at the waist and upper edge if the fabric is soft. Make three or four stitches on the underside of the frill, through the bodice.

8. *Hem.* Mark the hemline and trim according to which hem finish you select. A full short skirt could have a hand-sewn or machined hem of up to 2 cm ($\frac{3}{4}$ in) depth. Press the dress.

FLOUNCY BLOUSE WITH SKIRT

In this two-piece outfit, a hip-length, cap-sleeved blouse with a flounce neckline is worn tucked into a straight skirt. The blouse is made in an exquisite jade green silk Jacquard with a small satin spot; the perfect foil is a plain black skirt.

This version of the blouse features a V at the front and a round back neck, with the full flounce gathered and attached with binding. The skirt is short and straight and has a lining. The zip is in the left side seam.

Blouse

Fabric
90 cm (36 in) silk Jacquard

Size		
12	2.20 m	(2½ yd)
14	2.20 m	(2½ yd)
16	2.20 m	(2½ yd)
18	2.30 m	(2½ yd)
20	2.40 m	(2⅔ yd)

Haberdashery
Thread: 1 reel

Cutting out
Cap-sleeve pattern (full-size):
1 × back, to fold, round neck
1 × front, to fold, round neck
1 × 2.5 cm (1 in) bias strip for the neckline, to length given on page 36.
Circular flounce (measurements, page 52) × 6

Mark the V-neck on the front but do not cut.

Sewing
1. *Seams.* With RS together, stitch the side seams from hem to armhole with French seams or other seam suitable for soft, fraying fabric. Stitch and press the shoulder seams in the same way.
2. *Hem and sleeve hems.* Turn a narrow hem to WS round the bottom of the blouse, baste, press

lightly and slip hem. Make matching hems on the sleeves.

3. *Flounce.* Each circle of fabric should be cut through. Insert a gathering thread along each inner edge. Join them all together, end to end, with narrow French seams. Roll a narrow hem round the outer edge of the entire flounce and slip hem. Press the hem. Pass the bias strip through a tape maker and press the strip as it emerges folded.

Try on the blouse and check the depth of the V-neck. Raise the marking if necessary. Divide the neckline into four, marking CB and CF and two points along the V-neck. Divide the raw edge of the flounce into four. Place the flounce against the neckline WS down on RS blouse. Match the four quarter marks and pin. Pull up each gathering thread until the flounce fits the neckline. Secure the ends of the gathers, even out and baste all round the neck. Open out one fold of the binding, and place this RS down on RS flounce with the crease on the line of gathering. Beginning at one shoulder and leaving an end for joining, baste through the binding, flounce and blouse. Make a join in the binding, opening it out flat and folding back each end until the two folds meet. Slipstitch together and trim off the surplus. Stitch the bias strip to the blouse, following the crease in the binding; even out the gathers

where necessary. Remove the basting and any gathering thread that shows. Trim all raw edges to 5 mm ($\frac{1}{4}$ in); this is where the V-neck is cut to shape.

To complete, roll the folded binding to the inside of the blouse, bringing the fold onto the machine stitching. Baste flat and hem all round.

Skirt

Fabric
115 cm (45 in) fabric

Size		Lining	
12	90 cm (1 yd)		80 cm ($\frac{7}{8}$ yd)
14	90 cm (1 yd)		80 cm ($\frac{7}{8}$ yd)
16	1.60 m ($1\frac{3}{4}$ yd)		1 m ($1\frac{1}{8}$ yd)
18	1.60 m ($1\frac{3}{4}$ yd)		1 m ($1\frac{1}{8}$ yd)
20	1.60 m ($1\frac{3}{4}$ yd)		1 m ($1\frac{1}{8}$ yd)

Haberdashery
Thread: 2 reels
Fastening: 1 large hook and bar; 1 large press stud *or* 1 button
Heavy Fold-a-Band: waist length plus 2.5 cm (1 in) overlap
Zip: 20 cm (8 in)

Cutting out
Skirt (full-size pattern), lengthened to measurements given on page 37:
1 × back, to fold
1 × front, to fold
    Allocate space for the waistband to be cut later. Shorten the pattern by folding back 6 cm ($2\frac{1}{2}$ in) and cut:
1 × back, to fold, in lining
1 × front, to fold, in lining
    Mark the darts, front tucks and zip point.

Sewing
1. *Darts.* Fold back WS out and bring the dart lines together. Baste and stitch the darts. Press towards CB.

2. *Seams.* With back and front RS together, baste the side seams, leaving a zip opening at the left waist. Try on the skirt and adjust the side seams if necessary. Ignore the waist fitting for the moment. Stitch the seams. Using a large straight stitch, sew from the zip point to the waist along the zip opening. Press the seams open and neaten the edges. If you are

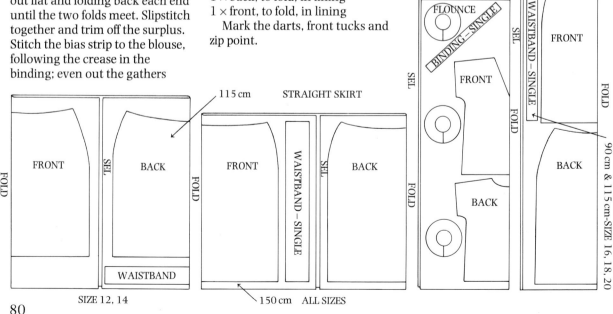

CAP-SLEEVE TOP, V-NECK & FLOUNCE

FLOUNCE

BINDING – SINGLE

FRONT

FRONT

WAISTBAND – SINGLE

BACK

BACK

SEL

FOLD

90 cm & 115 cm – SIZE 16, 18, 20

FRONT   WAISTBAND – SINGLE   BACK

SEL   SEL   FOLD

WAISTBAND

FOLD   SIZE 12, 14

115 cm   STRAIGHT SKIRT

150 cm   ALL SIZES

adding a lining, there is no need to neaten the edges above thigh level unless the fabric frays very badly.

3. *Zip.* Apply basting tape to the upper side of the zip tapes and remove the backing strip. Place the zip RS down over the pressed seam, with the teeth centred over the seamline and the slider 2 cm ($\frac{3}{4}$ in) below the waist edge. Press in place with your fingers. Stitch the zip by hand or machine parallel with the seamline, not too close to the teeth or the fabric will be pulled off the teeth. Stitch with the skirt RS up; do not sew across the bottom or a bulge will result. If you can, stitch from the base of zip to the waist on both sides. Press the stitching carefully with the tip of the iron. Remove the stitching in the seam.

4. *Waistband.* Measure Fold-a-Band around your waist and mark with fabric pen. Add 2.5 cm (1 in) overlap and cut. Place Fold-a-Band on WS fabric, matching perforations to SG. Press in place, using a warm iron and damp cloth. Cut out around the outside edge of the Fold-a-Band, adding 1.5 cm ($\frac{5}{8}$ in) at each end and allowing a little extra along the sides beyond the Fold-a-Band 1 cm ($\frac{3}{8}$ in) seam allowance.

5. With the skirt RS out and the zip open, place the waistband against the waist edge WS up. Beginning at the zip edge at the back, matching the perforations to the skirt seamline, and leaving 1.5 cm ($\frac{5}{8}$ in) extending beyond the zip, pin the band to the skirt. Hold the waistband taut and ease the skirt onto it.

When you reach the side seam, move to the front zip edge. Allow 4 cm ($1\frac{5}{8}$ in) of band to extend beyond the zip and pin. Fold the front tucks in position, towards CF, so that the skirt lies flat against the waistband but with a little ease. Pin the remainder of the waistband, close the zip and check the level of the band. Baste firmly along the perforated line. Try on the skirt, and adjust the waist level and tucks if necessary.

With the waistband uppermost, stitch along the perforations, fastening off securely across the top of the zip. Remove the basting. Fold the band up to extend beyond the top of the skirt and press. Fold along the perforations, RS out.

6. *Hem.* Try on the skirt, overlap and pin the waistband, and mark the overlap with fabric pen. Check the skirt length and mark the hem level. With the skirt WS out, fold up the hem surplus an even amount and pin at CB, CF and the side seams. Turn the skirt RS out and fold it with the side seams together, to check the seam lengths are equal. Fold up the hem all round and baste close to the fold. If you want to check the skirt length, insert a few pins in the hem surplus and try on the skirt. Press the hem along the fold. Trim the hem depth to an even amount all round for a deep hem. Neaten the raw edge and finish by hand with catch stitch under the edge. If your fabric is suitable for Wundaweb, the hem depth must be 3 cm ($1\frac{1}{4}$ in).

7. *Lining.* Stitch darts and seams as for the skirt, incorporating any adjustments made and leaving an opening for the zip 2 cm ($\frac{3}{4}$ in) longer than marked on the right seam. Press the lining and press back seam allowances at the zip opening of just under 2.5 cm (1 in). Snip the lining at an angle at the base of the opening and fold back. Fold up the hem edge twice and pin. Check with the skirt that the lining will be at least 2 cm ($\frac{3}{4}$ in) shorter then press the hem all round. Slip hem or machine to finish; a decorative stitch can be used. Lace edging may be attached at this stage, although remember to allow for its depth.

With the skirt WS out, slip the lining RS out over it. Match the seams, darts, zip edges and CF, and pin. Make sure the lining is well clear of the zip teeth then baste it to the zip tape along each side of the zip.

8. Ease the lining onto the skirt at the waist, folding the front tucks into place. Check that the lining and skirt hem are parallel then baste the lining to the seam allowance at the waist. To attach the lining, work by hand back stitch along the waist seamline, stitching through the lining and sinking the needle deeply into the seam allowances. Hem the lining to the zip tape.

Trim the waist seam allowances. Fold the waistband RS together at the ends and stitch across. Trim the corners and turn RS out. Bring the free edge of the waistband onto the back of the waist seam to cover the seam allowances. Fold under the edge of the waistband and baste it to the skirt. At the overlap, fold in both edges to meet. Hem the waistband to the skirt or machine all round from RS.

If the fabric is bulky, you may prefer to neaten the free edge of the waistband and let it lie flat over the inside of the skirt before stitching either all round or just along the waist seam.

9. *Finishing.* Attach a hook and bar at the marked position, at the inner end of the waistband overlap, and buttonhole stitch for strength. Alternatively, work a buttonhole in the overlap and sew a button to correspond. Work a 2.5 cm (1 in) bar tack at each seam 10 cm (4 in) above the hem to secure the lining. Press the skirt.

HALTER TOP WITH TROUSERS

These easy-fit trousers and flattering halter top are casual yet glamorous. The top is made in woven gold tissue fabric, the trousers in black woven polyester satin with a shell design.

The halter top is lined to the edge, the back neck strap has elastic in it and the side fastens with hooks and eyes on tape. The gold rose is made from scraps of fabric. The straight-legged trousers have elastic through the waist. A shaped belt in the same fabric is worn with them.

Halter top

Fabric
115 cm (45 in) wide woven gold tissue fabric

Size		
12	1.20 m ($1\frac{1}{2}$ yd)	
14	1.20 m ($1\frac{1}{2}$ yd)	
16	1.40 m ($1\frac{2}{3}$ yd)	
18	1.40 m ($1\frac{2}{3}$ yd)	
20	1.50 m ($1\frac{3}{4}$ yd)	

Haberdashery
Thread: 1 reel
Hook and eye tape: 20 cm (8 in)
Elastic: 13 mm ($\frac{1}{2}$ in) wide × 30 cm ($11\frac{1}{2}$ in)

Cutting out
Strapless bodice (full-size pattern): 2 × back, to fold, in fabric *or* 1 fabric and 1 lining
4 × halter front (diagram pattern, page 41) *or* 2 fabric and 2 lining
1 × halter strap, to measurements given on page 41

Mark the dots on the CF seam and shoulder pleats.

Sewing
1. *Strap.* Fold the fabric RS together, stitch the long edge and turn the strap RS out. Press. Thread the elastic through, pulling the ends out so that the fabric is slightly gathered. Stitch across each end of the strap to secure the elastic.
2. *Front.* Insert gathering threads between the dots along each edge of the CF seam, and neaten to prevent fraying. Fold the inverted pleat at the shoulder on RS and stitch across to secure.
3. *Front lining.* Stitch the CF seam and shoulder pleats as for the front.
4. *Back.* Join the back halter to the front, RS together, along the right side seam only. Join the back lining to the front lining along the right seam, holding the fabric WS away from you.
5. *Attaching the lining.* Arrange the lining RS up and place the halter RS down on top. Match and pin the seams and edges. Baste and stitch along the lower edge across the back and front. Baste and stitch the upper edge from the left seam along the top and up the armhole edge on the right and left sides, but stop the stitching 1.5 cm ($\frac{5}{8}$ in) from the shoulder.

At the raw edges of the neck, stitch the lining to the halter, starting exactly at the end of the CF seam, and stitching and sewing to within 1.5 cm ($\frac{5}{8}$ in) of the shoulder. Repeat on the second side of the neck. Remove all basting. Trim and snip all seam allowances. At the shoulders, press back the end of the fabric onto WS of the halter. Repeat with the ends of the lining. Turn the halter RS out, roll all the seams to the edge and press.
6. *Hooks and eyes.* Fold under the seam allowance on the back of the halter. Attach the eyes to the back of the halter. Cut the tape to length and insert it under the folded edge so that the edges extend. Baste in position or secure with basting tape. Machine along the tape. Fold under the edge of the lining onto the back of tape, and hem or machine in place.

On the front of the halter, fold in the raw edges to meet each other and slipstitch together. Place the hook tape 1.5 cm ($\frac{5}{8}$ in) back from the edge on WS. Baste in place. Try on the halter and adjust the position if necessary. Stitch the tape to the halter, sewing through all layers.
7. *Strap.* Insert the ends of the strap into the open ends of the halter. Baste through all layers. Try on and adjust. Stitch securely across the halter and through the strap.
8. *Rose.* See page 118 for instructions.

Trousers

Fabric
115 cm (45 in) wide polyester satin

Size		
12	2.50 m (3 yd)	
14	2.50 m (3 yd)	
16	2.50 m (3 yd)	
18	2.50 m (3 yd)	
20	2.60 m ($3\frac{1}{4}$ yd)	

Haberdashery
Thread: 1 reel
Elastic: 2.5 cm (1 in) wide × waist length
Wundaweb: 90 cm (36 in), for hems if required

Cutting out
Trousers (full-size pattern), lengthened as described on page 38:
2 × trouser pattern

Sewing
1. *Leg seams.* Fold each trouser leg RS together, matching the inside leg seam edges. Baste and stitch from crutch to hem. Neaten

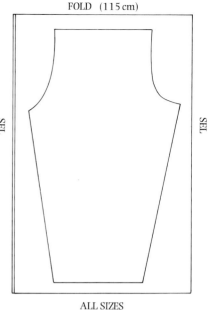

FOLD (115 cm)

SEL

SEL

ALL SIZES

HALTER TOP

NECK STRAP

FRONT

BACK

FRONT

BACK

SEL

FOLD

SEL

SIZE 12, 14

NECK STRAP

FRONT

BACK

FRONT

BACK

FOLD

SIZES 16, 18, 20

the edges and press the seams open.

2. *Crutch seam*. With legs RS out, match the leg seams with fabric RS together. Baste from the leg seam to the waist on front and back. Try on and adjust the crutch seam if necessary. Stitch the seam twice for strength. Neaten the raw edges and press the seam open from the waist down to the curve of the crutch.

Do not snip the seam allowances as it weakens the seam around the crutch.

3. *Waist casing*. Neaten the waist edge of the trousers. Fold over 3 cm ($1\frac{1}{4}$ in) onto the inside, baste and press. Stitch around the top of the trousers 5 mm ($\frac{1}{4}$ in) inside the neatened edge, leaving a 2.5 cm (1 in) gap at the back seam.

Insert the elastic and pull up to size. Overlap the ends and join securely. Complete the casing stitching.

It is useful to mark which is the back of trousers of this style, so use a contrast colour thread in the bobbin when you are stitching up the gap in the casing.

4. *Hems*. Turn up 3 cm ($1\frac{1}{4}$ in) to the inside of the trousers and baste. Try on and adjust the length. Neaten the raw edges of the hems. Complete by machining, slipstitching or inserting Wundaweb under the hem allowance. The hem must be well pressed with a warm iron on a damp cloth to make the Wundaweb adhere. It is wise to try it first on a spare piece of fabric. Press the trousers.

5. *Belt*. This is made from a shaped waistband. The diagram pattern and instructions are on page 60.

83

STRAP DRESS WITH FLOUNCE AND BAG

This elegant, eye-catching dress has a camisole top and a deep hemline circular flounce. It is made up in two shades of sea green wild silk. Both colours are used for the beaded Suffolk Puffs that dangle from the neckline and cluster on the bag.

The upper edge of the dress is bound and the zip is in the left side seam. The dress is unlined, but it would be a simple matter to make the same shape in lining fabric, sew the two together at the neck and armhole, and bind over both layers.

Fabric
115 cm (45 in) wide wild silk
All sizes, dress and bag:
main colour   contrast
2.40 m ($2\frac{1}{4}$ yd)   3.50 m ($3\frac{3}{4}$ yd)

Haberdashery
Thread: 2 reels
Zip: 40 cm (16 in)
Hook and eye: 1, for the top of the zip
Beads: for the Suffolk Puffs

Cutting out
Dress (full-size camisole pattern), lengthened as described on page 33:
1 × front, to fold
1 × back, to fold
2.5 cm (1 in) bias strips, cut to lengths given on page 33:
1 for the front neck
1 for the back neck
2 for the armholes/straps
Flounce (diagram pattern, page 51):
6 × quarter circle pattern, to fold
    Mark darts on the dress front.
Bag (diagram pattern, page 70): See page 70 for cutting out and making instructions.
    The Suffolk Puffs are made from scraps of fabric and are required early on in construction. Instructions for making them are on page 122.

Sewing
1. *Darts.* Fold RS together, bringing the sides of each dart together. Baste and stitch. Press flat then downwards.
2. *Seams.* With RS together, baste the dress front and back along the side seams, leaving 43 cm (17 in) open at the top of the left seam. Fit and adjust the seams then stitch, neaten and press. Trim 1.5 cm ($\frac{5}{8}$ in) from the neck and armhole edges to allow for the depth of the binding.
3. *Zip.* On the front of the dress, fold under 1.5 cm ($\frac{5}{8}$ in) and press. Snip the seam allowance halfway through at intervals along the curved part. On the back, fold under 1 cm ($\frac{3}{8}$ in) and press. Place the zip RS up under this edge, with the fold close beside the teeth and the slider 1 cm ($\frac{3}{8}$ in) below the raw edge at the armhole. Baste and stitch along the edge of the fabric by hand or machine. On the inside, snip the seam allowance to allow the fabric to lie flat. Snip the zip tape, if necessary, level with the waist then immediately oversew the cut edges of the seam allowance to prevent them fraying.

Overlap the front edge on to the zip, matching the upper edges, and secure with basting tape. Anchor the fabric in place at intervals, matching the folded edge to the stitching and retaining the shape of the seam. Baste along the zip and stitch close to the teeth. Remove the tape and basting stitches. Press the stitching.
4. *Suffolk Puffs.* Group in threes: large, medium and small. Join each set of three with a double thread run loosely through the puffs from one to another so that they are about 1 cm ($\frac{3}{8}$ in) apart. Use thread that matches the background fabric. The visible thread could be covered with loop stitch.

Place the puffs on RS front neckline, one set level with each point, one at CF, and the other two between. Anchor with basting tape at the top. Work a small bar tack under the middle puff of each set to attach it to the dress beneath, to prevent them twisting. Arrange the remaining puffs on the flap of the bag and stitch in place.
5. *Binding and straps.* Pass all bias strips through a small-size tape maker and press. Fold again and press. Place the front binding RS up on WS dress neck, overlapping them so that the raw edge of the dress reaches the central fold of the binding. Baste and stitch along the edges of the binding. Trim the raw edges, bring the remaining edge of the binding over to RS dress, on top of the ends of the puffs, and baste flat. Stitch along the edge of the binding using a straight stitch or, if you prefer, a small zigzag or decorative stitch. Press the binding but not the puffs.

Bind the back neck in the same way.

Bind the left armhole, applying the binding to WS above the zip and starting at the back armhole. Leave a seam allowance extending at the armhole. Attach the binding to the front armhole, starting at the other end of the strip. Stitch and trim the raw edges.

Bring the remaining edge of the binding onto RS dress, fold in the

ends above the zip and baste. Fold
WS together to form a strap above
the armhole sections. To finish the
right armhole, join the ends of the
binding together and press open.
Match the seam to the underarm
seam of the dress, place the
binding on WS, stitch and finish
the strap and binding as for the
left side.

Take care to check that both
straps are the same length before
stitching. To check the length of
the straps, pin them to the upper
edge of the dress and try it on
before stitching. Slipstitch the
ends of the binding. Attach a hook
and eye to fasten the binding at
the top of the zip.

6. *Flounce.* Insert a gathering
thread along the concave edge of
each piece of flounce. Join all the
seams with the fabric RS together.
Neaten and press the seams. Fold
a narrow hem all round the outer
edge and machine stitch. Press.

7. *Attaching the flounce.* Try on
the dress and check the length,
adding on the finished depth of
the flounce. If the dress needs to
be shortened, cut it off at the
lower edge. Divide dress and
flounce edges into four.

With the dress RS out, put the
flounce on it RS down, matching
the four points to the dress. Pin at
these points. Pull up each
gathering thread until the flounce
lies flat on the dress. Anchor the
thread ends and even out the
gathers in each section. Pin again
at intervals. Baste and stitch to
attach the flounce to the dress,
sewing with the gathers
uppermost so that they can be
kept even. Trim the raw edges and
neaten with zigzag. Press the
dress but not the puffs.

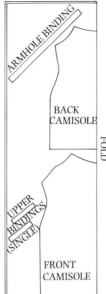

MAIN
CUT BAG FROM
SCRAPS

CONTRAST

STRAP DRESS
WITH FLOUNCE

TUNIC AND SKIRT

(See photograph on page 75.)
A three-quarter length tunic with a short skirt makes a simple day outfit. The border of cutwork above the tunic hem is repeated on the hat and bag. Crisp pure linen with a crease-shedding finish is a perfect choice of fabric.

Tunic

Fabric
115 cm (45 in) wide pure Irish linen
Tunic and bag:

Size	12	2.40 m (2¾ yd)
	14	2.40 m (2¾ yd)
	16	2.50 m (3 yd)
	18	2.50 m (3 yd)
	20	2.50 m (3 yd)

Haberdashery
Thread: 2 reels, plus 2 reels contrast Anchor Machine Embroidery thread No. 30

Cutting out
Cap-sleeve pattern (full-size):
1 × back, to fold, round neck, lengthened as described on page 36
1 × front, to fold, round neck, lengthened as described on page 36
1 × 2.5 cm (1 in) bias strip × 67 cm (26 in), for the neckline
Bag (see diagram pattern, page 69)

Mark CF and CB on the tunic hemline. Mark the top of the side slits 34 cm (13½ in) above the lower edge.

Sewing
1. *Cutwork.* See page 121 for cutwork preparation and stitching. Work the border, starting at least 8 cm (3¼ in) above the hem edge.
2. *Hem.* Turn up a 3 cm (1¼ in) hem on the front and back. Press, neaten and catch stitch, or secure with Wundaweb.

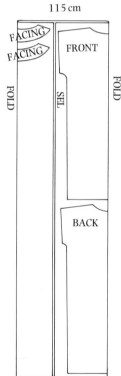

CUT BAG FROM SCRAPS
115 cm

TUNIC
SKIRT see p. 81

3. *Seams.* With hems level and RS together, baste along the side seams including the side slits. Baste the shoulder seams. Try on the tunic and adjust the side seams if necessary. Check the size of the neckline. If it needs enlarging, either make it slightly wider on the shoulder or stop the stitching on one shoulder seam a short distance from the neck edge to make an opening. (See page 124 on buttons and loops.) Stitch, press and neaten the side and shoulder seams.
4. *Side slits.* Press back the seam allowances and secure with catch stitch or narrow pieces of Wundaweb. At the hem, loop stitch neatly over the edge.
5. *Armholes.* Make a 1.5 cm (⅝ in) hem all round and finish with two parallel rows of stitching.
6. *Neckline.* Pass the bias strip through a tape maker and open out one fold. Apply to RS neckline, RS down, starting at a shoulder seam and leaving 2 cm (¾ in) to join. Baste the binding to the neckline. To join, press back the ends on SG at an angle of 45 degrees, so that they meet. Lift up the ends and hold RS together. Match the folds and stitch across the binding. Trim the ends and press the join. Stitch all round the neck, trim and snip the raw edges. Using the tip of the iron, press the binding to extend beyond the neck then roll it to the inside. Baste close to the edge then baste the remaining edge of the binding flat to dress. Finish by working two rows of stitching to match the armholes. Press the dress.

Skirt

See page 37 for requirements and sewing instructions, omitting the lining if preferred.

JACKET WITH FLOUNCE, CAMISOLE AND TROUSERS

A stunning but simple three-piece evening outfit, the camisole and trousers are made in purple polyester crêpe, the jacket in purple jersey with the surface glittering with paillettes. The neckline flounce is single. All the hems are machined for ease of handling.

Jacket

Fabric
150 cm (60 in) wide

Size	12	1.10 m ($1\frac{1}{3}$ yd)
	14	1.10 m ($1\frac{1}{3}$ yd)
	16	1.10 m ($1\frac{1}{3}$ yd)
	18	2.40 m ($2\frac{3}{4}$ yd)
	20	2.40 m ($2\frac{3}{4}$ yd)

Haberdashery
Thread: 1 reel
Shoulder pads: 1 pair Vilene medium-size pads
Soft Fold-a-Band: 41 cm (16 in), for the tops of the pockets

Cutting out
Jacket (full-size pattern):
1 × back, to fold
2 × front
2 × sleeve
Neckline flounce (diagram pattern, page 47) × 2
Pockets (measurements, page 35) × 2 (optional)

Mark CB jacket neck, the sleeve head point, the dot on the flounce and the corresponding dot on the jacket front.

Sewing
1. *Pockets (optional).* Press the Fold-a-Band to WS across the top of each pocket and zigzag the edge. Fold to RS along the perforations then stitch the ends 1.5 cm ($\frac{5}{8}$ in) from the edge. Snip

the corners, turn the pocket RS out, fold in the edge all round and baste. Stitch across the hem and press. Place the pockets on RS jacket front, 4 cm (1⅛ in) above the lower edge and 10 cm (4 in) from the front edge. Baste in position. Stitch round three sides to attach the pockets, either by hand with catch stitch under the edge or by machine. Fasten off the corners securely.

2. *Sleeves*. Fold WS out and stitch the seams. Press to one side, trim and zigzag or overlock. Zigzag or overlock the hem edge, turn up 3 cm (1¼ in) onto WS, baste and machine with a straight, decorative or jersey stitch that can be used on all the hems. Stitch with RS up for best finish. Note that the hem could be trimmed to 1 cm (⅜ in) before turning up.

3. *Seams*. Join the jacket fronts to the back along the side and shoulder seams. Finish and press as for the sleeve seam.

4. *Flounce*. With RS together, stitch the CB seam. This seam may be visible in wear so make a welt or decorative seam.

Turn a hem onto WS all round the outer edge of the flounce excluding the neck edge. Stitch to match the sleeve hem. Place the flounce to the jacket neck, matching the seam to CB, matching CF dots and with WS flounce to RS jacket. Baste and stitch the flounce to the jacket. Press the seam towards the jacket and trim the underneath seam allowance to 5 mm (¼ in).

5. *Hem*. Fold a 3 cm (1¼ in) hem onto WS along the lower edge and baste. This can either be finished with catch stitch as a deep hem, or it could be trimmed and finished to match the sleeves. To complete the neck edge, turn a narrow hem onto WS from the front corners to the flounce; from there, treat the neckline seam allowance in the same way. Stitch to match the edge of the flounce.

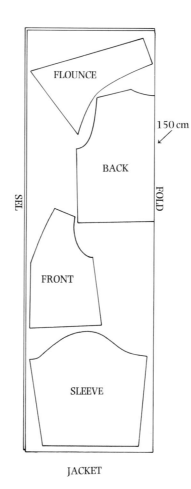

JACKET

6. *Sleeves*. With the jacket and sleeves RS out, select the right sleeve (the front armhole is more scooped) and insert it in the right armhole. Match the underarm seams and pin. Pin the sleeve to the armhole around the underarm section and baste. Turn the jacket WS out over the sleeve head so that the jacket is on top. Flip the sleeve head and jacket armhole edge to the outside, match the sleeve head point to the shoulder seam and pin. Pin between the end of the basting and the sleeve head and baste. Try the jacket on to check the length of the shoulder seam, and adjust if necessary. With the sleeve uppermost, stitch round the armhole. Trim and neaten the edges. Press the jacket and hang up.

7. *Shoulder pads*. Cut an oval shape of fabric or lining. Do not use the paillette jersey but the polyester crêpe would be suitable. The size of the pieces should be at least 5 cm (2 in) wider than the pad and twice its length. Fold the fabric RS out and slide the pad between the layers with the thick part against the fold. Pin or baste the upper layer to the pad and do the same underneath the pad; retain the shape by pulling the fabric tight. Machine round following the edge of the pad, trim the excess fabric and zigzag over the edge to finish. Insert the pad into the shoulder, the bigger part to the front of the jacket. Line up the central notch on the pad with the shoulder seam, but then move the pad 1 cm (⅜ in) further towards the front. Pin from the outside of the jacket through into the pad. On the inside, stitch in place with loose stitches, sewing the thick edge to the seam allowances. At the point of the pad, work a bar tack 1 cm (⅜ in) long between the pad and the shoulder seam.

Camisole

Fabric

115 cm (45 in) wide polyester crêpe

Size		
12	1.40 m	($1\frac{2}{3}$ yd)
14	1.40 m	($1\frac{2}{3}$ yd)
16	1.40 m	($1\frac{2}{3}$ yd)
18	1.50 m	($1\frac{3}{4}$ yd)
20	1.50 m	($1\frac{3}{4}$ yd)

Haberdashery

Thread: 1 reel
Zip: 40 cm (16 in)
Hook and eye: 1, for the top of the zip

Cutting out

Camisole (full-size pattern):
1 × back, to fold
1 × front, to fold
2.5 cm (1 in) bias strips, to lengths given on page 34:
1 for the front neck
1 for the back neck
2 for the armholes/straps
  Mark the darts on the camisole front.

Sewing

1. *Darts*. Fold the front RS together to bring the dart sides together. Baste, stitch and press the darts downwards. Trim 1.5 cm ($\frac{5}{8}$ in) off the neck and armholes to allow for the binding.
2. *Seams*. With the back and front RS together, stitch the right seam, press open and neaten. Stitch the left seam from the hem for a distance of 3 cm ($1\frac{1}{4}$ in). Press open and neaten the edges.

3. *Zip*. On the camisole front, fold under 1.5 cm ($\frac{5}{8}$ in) and press. The edge is curved so do this carefully, snipping into the edge once or twice at waist level. On the back, fold under 1 cm ($\frac{3}{8}$ in) and press. Place the zip under this edge with the fold close to the teeth and the slider 1 cm ($\frac{3}{8}$ in) below the armhole edge. Stitch the zip beside the teeth. Snip the seam allowance at the waist if necessary.
  Overlap the front pressed edge onto the zip, bringing the fold over the line of stitching. Match the edge at the top, and secure with strips of basting tape. Stitch beside the teeth from the armhole edge right to the bottom of the camisole.
4. *Hem*. Turn a narrow hem to WS camisole and finish by a method suitable for the fabric.
5. *Neckline*. Pass all the bias strips through a tape maker and press. Apply the binding to the front and back neck, keeping it folded, and baste to WS camisole. Machine along the folded edge to attach. Trim the raw edges, then bring the remaining edge of the binding onto RS so that it covers the stitching. Baste and machine in place along the edge of the binding. This could be a decorative stitch, even a hand embroidery stitch.

6. *Armholes*. Join the ends of one bias strip, press the join and refold the binding. Apply to WS right armhole, matching the join to the camisole seam. Stitch from the upper edge round the underarm. On the left armhole, apply the other strip to WS, starting at the top of the zip and leaving 1.5 cm ($\frac{5}{8}$ in) extending. Stitch in place and trim the raw edges. Fold back the ends and bring the remaining binding edge over onto RS on both armholes to cover the stitching. Baste to secure. To make the straps, baste the binding folded, with the edges together. From RS, stitch along the edge of the binding round the armhole and along the strap. Slipstitch across the ends of the binding above the zip. Sew a hook and eye to the binding. Press the camisole.

Trousers

Fabric

115 cm (45 in) wide polyester crêpe

Size		
12	2.50 m	(3 yd)
14	2.50 m	(3 yd)
16	2.50 m	(3 yd)
18	2.50 m	(3 yd)
20	2.60 m	($3\frac{1}{4}$ yd)

Haberdashery

Thread: 1 reel
Elastic: 2.5 cm (1 in) wide × waist length

Cutting out

Trousers (full-size pattern), lengthened as described on page 38:
2 × trouser pattern

Sewing

Follow steps 1–4 on pages 82–83, completing the hems with stitching to match the hem of the camisole.

CHESSBOARD BLOUSE WITH SKIRT

This hip-length cap-sleeved blouse with a flounce collar is worn with a long black velvet skirt with shaped waistband.

The blouse is in red, cream and black printed polyester. This version of the blouse has a V-back and a flounce attached with binding.

Blouse

Fabric
115 cm (45 in) polyester print

Size		
	12	2 m (2⅓ yd)
	14	2 m (2⅓ yd)
	16	2 m (2⅓ yd)
	18	2.10 m (2½ yd)
	20	2.10 m (2½ yd)

Haberdashery
Thread: 1 reel

Cutting out
See page 80 for cutting layout. Cap-sleeve pattern (full-size), back and front the same:
1 × back, to fold, cut round neck
1 × front, to fold, round neck
1 × 2.5 cm (1 in) bias strip, for the neckline, to length given on page 34
Circular flounce (measurements, page 52) × 6

Mark the V-neck on the back but do not cut.

Sewing
1. *Seams*. With RS together, stitch the side and shoulder seams, neaten the raw edges and press.
2. *Hems*. Turn narrow hems to WS around the hem and armholes, press and stitch. Try on the blouse and check the depth of the V at the back, adjusting the marking if necessary.
3. *Flounce*. Cut each circle through and insert a gathering thread along the inner edge of each. Join the circles end to end with narrow seams. Roll a narrow hem around the outer edge and stitch. Press.

Divide the blouse neckline into four. Divide the flounce into four and pin WS flounce to RS blouse, matching the quarters. Pull up the gathering threads until the flounce edge lies flat. Baste all round the neck.

Pass the bias strip through a tape maker and press. Apply the strip flat to WS blouse, starting at a shoulder seam and leaving an end to join. Baste all round. Join the ends of the strip by opening out and pressing back the ends to meet. Slipstitch the join and trim off the surplus. Refold and repress the strip. Stitch along the edge of the binding to attach it to the blouse. Trim the raw edges. Bring the remaining edge of the binding over onto RS blouse and baste so that the edge covers all the stitching. Machine along the edge of the binding with the blouse RS up.

Skirt
See page 37 for pattern details, and page 81 for making up instructions.

Shaped waistband
See page 60 for pattern details and making up instructions.

SHORT JACKET

A jacket is always useful to put over dresses and trousers, in matching or contrasting fabric. This version is made up in Jacquard taffeta, it is below waist in length, has three-quarter sleeves with fold-back cuffs, and is lined. The ruched trimming is made from silver ribbon.

Fabric

115 cm (45 in) wide taffeta

Size		
12	1.90 m	(2¼ yd)
14	2.10 m	(2⅓ yd)
16	2.10 m	(2⅓ yd)
18	2.30 m	(2½ yd)
20	2.30 m	(2½ yd)

Lining: 10 cm (4 in) less than above

Haberdashery

Thread: 2 reels
Sew-in or iron-on Vilene: 55 cm (21 in) × 20 cm (8 in)
Hook and eye: 1, for waist

Cutting out

For layout, see jacket, page 88. omitting the flounce.
Jacket (full-size pattern) to below-waist cutting line, in fabric and lining:
1 × back, to fold
2 × front
2 × sleeve (shorten the sleeve by folding back the cuff and cut the pattern pieces in lining)
   Mark the sleeve head point. Curve the front corners if desired.

Sewing

1. *Vilene.* Place the front jacket on the folded Vilene and cut out, following the front edge and shaping the opposite edge of the Vilene from mid-shoulder to mid-hem. Baste or press the Vilene to WS jacket fronts.
2. *Sleeves.* Fold RS together and stitch the seams, following the shape for the cuff. Snip the seam allowances at the cuff angles and press the seams open. Fold onto WS along the cuff foldline, and secure the raw edge to the sleeve with catch stitch, or with Wundaweb if suitable. Stitch and press the lining seams and turn WS out. Slip the lining inside the sleeve, WS together, and baste around the sleeve head and above the cuff. Fold under the lining raw edge onto the cuff edge, baste and hem.
3. *Shoulder seams.* With back and fronts RS together, stitch the shoulder seams and press open. Stitch and press the lining shoulder seams. With lining and jacket RS together, pin then stitch along the hem, front edge and back neckline. Stitch the jacket to the lining along the back hem. Snip and trim the seam allowances, turn RS out, roll all seams to the edge and press.
4. *Decorative edging.* Prepare sufficient ruching, zigzag trimming, etc. Place on RS jacket with the edges level. Stitch in place.
5. *Side seams.* Holding the jacket RS out, join the jacket and lining seam in one seam from armhole to armhole. Match the armhole edges and seams and keep fabric RS together. Stitch the seam from the armhole down to the hem and up to the armhole on each side. Press open and turn RS out through the open armholes.
6. *Armholes.* Baste through the jacket and lining round the armholes 5 cm (2 in) within the raw edges. Set the sleeves into the armholes, pinning and basting the sleeves to the jacket and excluding the lining. Stitch round the armholes and press the seam allowances towards the sleeves.

   Insert the shoulder pads between the lining and the jacket and oversew the edges to the seam allowance of each sleeve head. Fold under the raw edge of the lining and overlap it onto the armhole seam allowances. Pin in place, arranging it to ease evenly over each sleeve head. Hem all round the armholes. Press the jacket.

TRIANGULAR TOP

This pretty accessory is worn over one shoulder to top a dress or blouse. It is made here in soft black and gold lace.

Fabric
115 cm (45 in) wide lace fabric
Top and belt: 1.90 cm ($2\frac{1}{4}$ yd)

Haberdashery
Thread: 1 reel
Heavy Vilene: 20 cm ($\frac{1}{4}$ yd), for the belt
Elastic: 1 cm ($\frac{3}{8}$ in) × waist length
Hook and eye: 1 medium

Cutting out
Diagram pattern, page 43:
1 × front, to required length
1 × back, to the same length
1 × 3 cm ($1\frac{1}{4}$ in) bias strip × twice the width of the pattern at waist level, for the casing
Cut the front and back from single fabric with pattern RS up.

Sewing
1. *Side seam*. With fabric RS together, stitch the seam from underarm to hem. If the fabric is transparent, use a narrow or French seam. A side slit can be made by stitching from underarm to 3 cm ($1\frac{1}{4}$ in) below the casing line.
2. *Shoulder seam*. With RS out, fold and pin the shoulder tucks flat in the direction of the arrows; stitch to hold. Join the back to the front along the shoulder edge. Trim and neaten.
3. *Hems*. Make a narrow hem along the neck edge of the top and stitch. Make a hem to match along the lower edge, folding in the points neatly before stitching. On the armholes, turn narrow hems, snipping at the underarm so that the hem lies flat. (The edges of net can simply be trimmed; on other fine fabrics and lace, a small zigzag stitch would produce a picot edge. This finish would eliminate the problem of making the points neat.)
4. *Casing*. Either zigzag or overlock the long edges of the casing strip or pass it through a large-size tape maker to fold it. Apply the casing strip flat to WS top, folding in the ends 1 cm ($\frac{3}{8}$ in) from the front edge. Stitch along each long side. Thread the elastic through the casing, and secure one end with stitching.

5. *Fastening*. Attach the hook to the front edge of the top, level with the casing; attach the eye to the back or edge. Put the top on, fasten the hook and pull up the elastic to fit. Trim the end of the elastic and stitch in place to secure.

Belt
See page 58 for pattern details and making up instructions.

94

BODICE WITH SEPARATE PEPLUM

This boned bodice can be worn on its own or with a separate wrapover peplum over a skirt. The fabric used here is white moiré taffeta, self-lined. Instructions below include a wide, shaped strap which is optional; and there is opportunity for beading or elaborate stitching of the garment.

Fabric
115 cm (45 in) moiré taffeta
All sizes, bodice and peplum:
1.50 m (1¾ yd)

Haberdashery
Thread: 2 reels
Rigilene boning: 80 cm (31 in)
Heavy Fold-a-Band: waist length plus 5 cm (2 in)
Velcro: 4 cm (1½ in)
Hook and eye tape: 20 cm (8 in)
Iron-on Vilene: for the strap, to size shown on page 67 (optional)

Cutting out
Bodice (full-size pattern):
2 × CF panel, to fold
4 × side front panel
2 × back, to fold
2 × strap, to size shown on page 67 (optional)
1 × 2.5 cm (1 in) × 90 cm (36 in) bias strip, for the boning
Peplum pattern page 50:
4 × quarter circular skirt sections

Sewing

BODICE
1. Follow instructions 1–4 on pages 73–74, omitting the instruction to gather the CF panel.
2. *Lining.* Place the hook and eye tape, with eyes attached, on RS of the back bodice with the tape on the seamline and the edges towards the bodice. Stitch the tape. Fold the lining over the bodice so that both are WS out. Baste and stitch together along the lower edge and across each end, leaving a gap in the lower edge. Trim the corners and snip the curves. Press back the edges of the gap. Turn the bodice RS out. Slipstitch along the gap. Roll the seams to the edge and press.
3. *Fastening.* Place the hook side of the tape under the front edge 1.5 cm (⅝ in) inside the edge and machine along each edge of the tape.

STRAP (optional)
1. Iron the Vilene to WS of one piece of the strap. Decorate the strap as desired.
2. Place both pieces of the strap RS together. Baste and stitch round the outer edge but not across the narrow end. Snip the seam allowance and turn the strap RS out. Roll the join to the edge and press.
3. Zigzag or overcast the strap end. Pin and stitch inside the upper edge of the bodice on the left side, then bring the decorated end to overlap the bodice front on the right side. Adjust the length. Slipstitch in position.

PEPLUM
1. With RS together, stitch all seams except one, neaten and press open. Fold and stitch narrow hems along remaining edges.
2. Fold and stitch a narrow hem around the outer edge of the peplum.
3. Press the Fold-a-Band to WS fabric and cut out round it. Check the amount of overlap and mark. Fold the band RS together and stitch across the ends, snip the corners and turn RS out. Sew the Velcro in position, the soft side on the outer part and the firm side on the underlap, so that it fits your waist when fastened.
4. Fold in both long edges along the perforations and press the band folded.
5. Insert the waist edge of the peplum between the waistband edges, baste and stitch all round from RS. The peplum may be attached to the waist of the bodice if you wish. (Follow instruction 3 on page 74.)

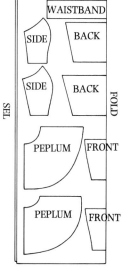

STRAPLESS TOP
PEPLUM
115 cm/45 in

SHORT SKIRT WITH BASQUE

(See photograph on page 103.)
This attractive short skirt has
gathered sections below a low
yoke. It is made in red moiré
taffeta and unlined; the zip is in
the left side seam. The straight
skirt pattern and the gathered
skirt are combined for this design.
It could also be made ankle
length.

Fabric
115 cm (45 in) wide moiré taffeta

Size		
12	2.50 m	(3 yd)
14	2.50 m	(3 yd)
16	2.80 m	(3¼ yd)
18	2.80 m	(3¼ yd)
20	2.80 m	(3¼ yd)

Haberdashery
Thread: 2 reels
Zip: 20 cm (8 in)
Fold-a-Band: waist length plus
5 cm (2 in), plus 3 cm (1¼ in) seam
allowance
Velcro: 4 cm (1½ in)

Cutting out
Skirt (full-size pattern):
1 × back, to fold, not lengthened
1 × front, to fold, not lengthened
    Allocate space for a waistband
to be cut later.
Gathered skirt (diagram pattern,
page 53):
4 × panels, to fold, upper edge B
and hemline E
    Mark the darts, tucks, zip point,
CF and CB.

Sewing
1. Follow steps 1–5 on
pages 80–81.
2. *Gathered section.* With RS
together, stitch the seams to join
the four panels together. Press
and neaten. Insert a gathering
thread along the upper edge of
each panel.
3. *Hip join.* With upper skirt RS

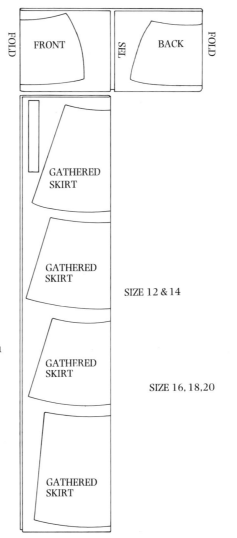

SHORT SKIRT WITH BASQUE

out and lower section WS out,
slide one over the other and
match the raw edges. Match the
side seams and CF and CB to the
lower skirt seams. Pin, pull up the
gathers and anchor the thread
ends. Baste all round. Try on the
skirt and mark the hemline, at the
same time checking that the hip
seam is at a suitable level.
4. Stitch the hip seam, trim the

edges and neaten. Turn up the
hem, neaten the raw edge and
secure with catch stitch under the
edge. Alternatively, turn a narrow
hem and finish with machine
stitching.
5. Attach the Velcro to the
waistband, sewing the firm side to
face outwards from the body and
using hemming or zigzag stitch.
Press the skirt.

COAT AND DRESS

This beautifully elegant outfit consists of a three-quarter-length coat over a camisole-top dress.

The dress is made in blue and black satin-striped polyester voile, and is lined. The coat is in petrel-blue shot chiffon and has long sleeves and a flounce collar.

Coat

Fabric

115 cm (45 in) wide chiffon

Size	12	4 m ($4\frac{1}{2}$ yd)
	14	4.10 m ($4\frac{2}{3}$ yd)
	16	4.30 m ($4\frac{3}{4}$ yd)
	18	4.30 m ($4\frac{3}{4}$ yd)
	20	4.40 m (5 yd)

Haberdashery

Thread: 2 reels

Cutting out (see following page)
Jacket (full-size pattern), lengthened as shown on page 35:
1 × back, to fold
2 × front
2 × sleeve
2 × flounce (diagram pattern, page 47)

Mark the sleeve head point, and the dots on the jacket front and the flounce.

Sewing

Follow instructions 2–6 on page 88, but using seam and hem finishes that are suitable for chiffon.

It would be wise to delay stitching the coat hem until it can be tried on over the dress.

99

Dress

Fabric

115 cm (45 in) wide striped voile
All sizes: 2.50 m (3 yd)
115 cm (45 in) wide lining

Size	12–18	2.30 m (2⅔ yd)
	20	2.40 m (2¾ yd)

Haberdashery

Thread: 2 reels, plus 1 to match
the lining
Zip: 40 cm (16 in)
Lace edging (optional): 1.20 m
(1⅓ yd), for the hem of the lining
Hook and eye: 1, for the top of the
zip

Cutting out

Camisole (full-size pattern),
lengthened as shown on page 34:
1 × back, to fold; also in lining but
3 cm (1¼ in) shorter
1 × front, to fold; also in lining but
3 cm (1¼ in) shorter
2.5 cm (1 in) wide bias strips, to
lengths given on page 34:
2 × armhole binding
1 × front neck binding
1 × back neck binding
   Mark the bust darts.

Sewing

1. Follow instructions 1–2 on
page 89.
2. *Lining*. Stitch the darts and
seams and press, leaving a zip
opening of 46 cm (18 in) in the
right seam. Snip the seam
allowances at the base of the
opening and press back 2 cm (¾ in)
onto WS right up to the armhole.
Snip the edge of the lining so that
the edges lie flat. Turn up a 3 cm
(1¼ in) hem onto WS and stitch
decoratively; or, if you are
attaching lace, shorten the lining
appropriately. Press the lining and
put inside the dress with WS
together, match seams and edges,
and baste together. Baste the
lining to the zip tape, keeping the
edges well clear of the zip teeth.
Hem all round.
3. Follow instructions 4–5 on
page 89 to complete.

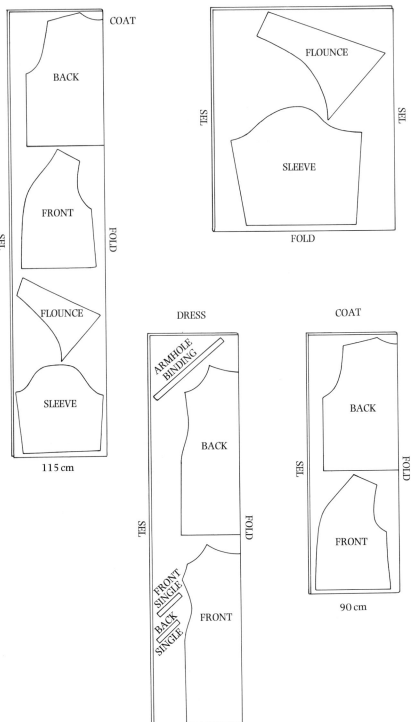

LONG SKIRT AND BLOUSE

A classic, elegant look for the evening is perfect in cream satin and black velvet. The sleeveless blouse has a flounce neck with the V at either front or back; the ankle-length velvet skirt has a shaped waistband and long hemline slit.

On fine fabrics and those that fray, the flounce on the blouse can be made double. It is extravagant of fabric, but the under layer could be made of lining which would reduce the amount of fabric required.

Blouse

Fabric

90 cm (36 in) silk satin

Size		
12	2.80 m	($3\frac{1}{4}$ yd)
14	2.80 m	($3\frac{1}{4}$ yd)
16	2.80 m	($3\frac{1}{4}$ yd)
18	2.90 m	($3\frac{1}{3}$ yd)
20	2.90 m	($3\frac{1}{3}$ yd)

115 cm (45 in) crêpe-back satin

Size		
12	2.10 m	($2\frac{1}{3}$ yd)
14	2.10 m	($2\frac{1}{3}$ yd)
16	2.10 m	($2\frac{1}{3}$ yd)
18	2.20 m	($2\frac{1}{2}$ yd)
20	2.20 m	($2\frac{1}{2}$ yd)

Haberdashery
Thread: 1 reel

Cutting out (see following page)
Cap-sleeve pattern (full-size), traced to cut-away armhole:
1 × back, to fold, cut round neck
1 × front, to fold, cut round neck
12 × circular flounce *or* 6 fabric and 6 lining, to measurements given on page 52
2.5 cm (1 in) wide bias strips, to lengths given on page 36:
1 × neck binding
2 × armhole binding
Mark the V-neck front but do not cut.

Sewing
1. *Seams and hem.* Follow instructions 1–2 on page 75.
2. *Armholes*. Pass the bias strips through a tape maker and press.

Starting at the underarm and leaving 1.5 cm ($\frac{5}{8}$ in) for joining, open out one fold and baste RS binding to RS armhole. Make the join level with the side seam by opening the binding flat and pressing back the ends to meet each other. Slipstitch the ends together and trim. Stitch all round the armhole to attach the binding. Trim the seam allowance, fold the binding onto WS blouse, baste and hem along the edge of the binding to finish.

3. *Flounce.* Cut into each circle. Join six end to end for the lining, with narrow seams; join the remaining six for the upper layer. Place both complete circles RS together, stagger the seams to avoid bulk and stitch round the outer edge. Snip and trim the raw edges and turn the flounce RS out. Roll the seam to the edge, baste and press. Alternatively, place the flounces WS together and stitch the outer raw edges with a decorative machine embroidery stitch, such as scallops.

Insert a gathering thread through both layers along the inner edge of each section.

Pass the bias strip through a tape maker and press. Attach the flounce and complete the blouse by following instruction 3 on page 80.

Long skirt

Fabric
122 cm (48 in) wide cotton velvet
Size		
12	1.40 m ($1\frac{2}{3}$ yd)
14	1.40 m ($1\frac{2}{3}$ yd)
16	2.50 m (3 yd)
18	2.50 m (3 yd)
20	2.50 m (3 yd)

115 cm (45 in) wide lining
Size		
12	1.20 m ($1\frac{1}{3}$ yd)
14	1.20 m ($1\frac{1}{3}$ yd)
16	2.30 m ($1\frac{1}{3}$ yd)
18	2.30 m ($1\frac{1}{2}$ yd)
20	2.30 m ($1\frac{1}{2}$ yd)

The velvet must be cut with the pile running all hem to waist or all waist to hem.

Haberdashery
Thread: 2 reels
Fastening: 1 large hook and bar, plus 1 press stud *or* 5 cm (2 in) Velcro
Heavy Vilene: for the shaped waistband
Zip: 20 cm (8 in)
Ribbon (optional): single satin 35 mm ($1\frac{3}{8}$ in) wide, for the side slit

Cutting out (see page 80)
Skirt (full-size pattern), lengthened as shown on page 37:
1 × back, to fold
1 × front, to fold
   Shorten the skirt pattern by 10 cm (4 in) and cut:
1 × back, to fold, in lining
1 × front, to fold, in lining
   Mark the darts, front tucks, zip point and the depth of the hemline slit required.
Shaped waistband (diagram pattern, page 60), to waist size:
2 × waistband *or* 1 fabric and 1 lining
1 × Vilene

Sewing
1. Construct the skirt following instructions 1–3 on page 80, but leaving a side slit in the left seam. Stitch all the seams in the direction of the pile of the velvet, not against it.
2. *Waistband.* Make the shaped waistband following the instructions for a straight waistband on page 81. Add decoration if required.
3. Follow instructions 5–8 on page 81 to complete the skirt. Finish the lining by folding under the raw edges alongside the side slit and hem in place. Attach the fastening to the waistband.

BLOUSE

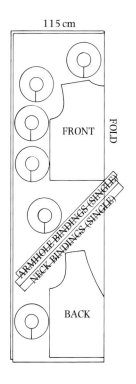

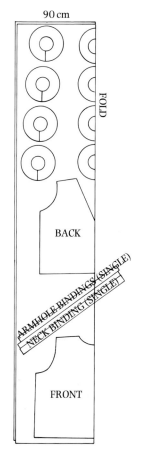

CAPE

Made in multi-coloured glitter jersey, this light evening wrap would be equally suitable for wearing over a dress or with trousers. The pattern is suitable for any soft, lightweight fabric.

Haberdashery

Thread: 1 reel
Elastic: 1 cm ($\frac{3}{8}$ in) wide; 2 × wrist length
Decoration for tie ends (optional): 2 silver beads

Cutting out

1 oval shape, as described on page 69, cut along CF
1 × 2.5 cm (1 in) bias strip, for the neckline

Sewing

1. *Hem.* Fold under and zigzag round the outer edge, excluding the neckline. Use a small stitch, let the stitch fall off the fold at the right and fold under the edge no more than 6 mm ($\frac{1}{4}$ in). Trim away the surplus fabric close to the stitching.

2. *Neckline.* Insert a gathering thread along the neckline and pull it up until the neck measures 45 cm ($17\frac{1}{2}$ in). Find the centre of the neckline and the centre of the bias strip, apply RS bias to RS neckline, and stitch round from CF to CF.

3. *Tie ends.* Make the tie ends by folding the strip RS together from CF edge to the end. Stitch along each tie. Trim the seam allowances of the ties and the neckline. Turn the ties RS out, using a rouleau needle. Fold under the raw edge along the neck and hem the fold to the machine stitching. Finish the tie ends by pushing the end 1 cm ($\frac{3}{8}$ in) back inside the tube. Gather up and sew a bead to the end if you wish.

4. *Inserting the elastic.* Cut the elastic to fit your wrists and join the ends together. Divide the elastic in half and mark. Fold the cape along the shoulders. Place the elastic on WS at the wrist edge, matching one mark to the fold. Attach with a wide zigzag or elastic stitch, stretching the elastic as you sew. Stop when you reach the halfway mark on the elastic and move straight on to the other edge. Complete the stitching, still stretching the elastic.

RUCHED AND TIERED DRESS

This pretty dance dress has a ruched, strapless, drop-waist bodice and a three-tier skirt. It is made in bright blue spotted net on a base of blue lining.

The skirt tiers are cut from measurements; the bodice is made from the strapless pattern, lengthened, with ruched panels on top.

Fabric

115 cm (45 in) wide net
All sizes: 5.20 m (5¾ yd)

115 cm (45 in) wide lining
All sizes: 3 m (3⅓ yd)

Haberdashery

Thread: 2 reels
Zip: 40 cm (16 in)
Rigilene boning: 127 cm (50 in)
Grosgrain ribbon: waist length, plus 5 cm (2 in) waist stay
Hooks and eyes: 2 small

Cutting out

NET
Ruched strapless bodice (diagram pattern, page 48):
1 × back, to fold
2 × side front
1 × CF, to fold
Skirt tiers, to measurements given on page 56:
3 × top tier
4 × middle tier
5 × lower tier

LINING
Strapless bodice (full-size pattern), lengthened to below waist as described on page 33:
2 × back to fold
4 × side front
2 × CF, to fold
1 × 2.5 cm (1 in) bias
strip × 1.40 m (1⅔ yd), for the boning

Gathered skirt panel, to measurements given on page 52:
4 × panels, to fold, to waistline A and hemline D
Mark placement lines B and C.

Sewing

LINING
1. *Bodice*. Make the bodice lining and insert the Rigilene as described in instruction 2 on page 73. Stitch across each end of the boning channels.
2. *Skirt*. With RS together, join the four panels together. Stitch, neaten and press the seams, leaving one open for 15 cm (6 in) below the waist.
   Turn up a narrow hem around the bottom of the skirt and machine, using a small zigzag or shell-effect stitch.

DRESS
1. *Bodice*. To mount net on to remaining lining insert gathering threads along all the long edges of the net bodice sections. Place each piece RS up on RS of the matching lining section, match the raw edges at the waist and upper edge, and pin. Pull up all the gathering threads until the net lies flat on the lining. Baste the net to the lining all round each section.
   Handling the net and lining pieces as one layer, complete the bodice as described on page 74, instructions 1–2.

RUCHED DRESS

115 cm net

RUCHED BACK

FOLD

RUCHED SIDE

RUCHED C.F.

Cut tiers with grain parallel to short ends.

115 cm LINING

SIDE

BACK

SIDE

BACK

GATHERED SKIRT

C.F.

GATHERED SKIRT

FOLD

GATHERED SKIRT

GATHERED SKIRT

2. *Skirt.* Construct the tiers, leaving the hems unfinished. Insert a gathering thread along the upper edge of each piece. With RS together, join all the bottom tier pieces together end to end. Divide into four. Divide the skirt into four at placement line C. Place the net tier RS up on RS lining, with the raw edge 1.5 cm ($\frac{5}{8}$ in) above the placement line, matching the quarters, and pin. Pull up the gathering threads until each section of net lies flat on the lining. Stitch the tiers to the lining with a line of stitching 1.5 cm ($\frac{5}{8}$ in) below the edge of the net.

Construct the middle tier in the same way and stitch to RS lining along placement line B.

Join the top tier pieces RS together, but on one seam stitch for 2 cm ($\frac{3}{4}$ in) only at the lower edge to leave space for the zip. Divide the tier into four. Place the top tier RS up on RS lining, matching the waist edges. Pin together at CF, CB and right seam. At the zip opening, fold under the edge of the net to lie on top of the folded edge of the lining, and pin.

Pull up the gathers until the net lies flat on the lining, then stitch 1.5 cm ($\frac{5}{8}$ in) below the waist edge.

Insert gathering threads in the waist edge of the skirt, through both net and lining, one thread to each lining panel.

3. *Waist join.* Join the bodice to the skirt at the waist, following instructions 5–6 on page 78.

4. *Zip.* Snip the bodice and lining seam allowances at the waist, press the seam allowances to WS and insert the zip. On the skirt, hold the net free and stitch the zip to the lining only. Follow the instructions on page 74, stitching the zip in two stages: first from the upper edge to the waist on the back and front bodice; then from the waist to the base of the zip on each side, holding the top tier of net free.

Attach the hooks and eyes at the top of the zip. Attach the waist stay. Press the skirt of the dress.

FRILLED SKIRT AND TOP

This evening outfit consists of a below waist strapless bodice with a narrow pleated frill along the upper edge, and a long skirt with a wide pleated frill cascading down the back. It is made in black and gold acetate grosgrain with black and gold striped net for the frills, which are edged with narrow black velvet ribbon.

Fabric
122 cm (48 in) wide acetate grosgrain
Strapless top, self-lined:
All sizes: 1.60 m (2 yd)
Skirt:

Size		
12	1.40 m	($1\frac{2}{3}$ yd)
14	1.40 m	($1\frac{2}{3}$ yd)
16	2.50 m	(3 yd)
18	2.50 m	(3 yd)
20	2.50 m	(3 yd)

122 cm (48 in) striped net
All sizes: 3.40 m ($3\frac{3}{4}$ yd)

Haberdashery
Thread: 3 reels
Hook and eye tape: 30 cm ($11\frac{3}{4}$ in)
Heavy Fold-a-Band: waist length plus 5 cm (2 in)
Rigilene boning: 127 cm (50 in)
Zip: 20 cm (8 in)
Velvet ribbon: 6 mm ($\frac{1}{4}$ in) wide and the following lengths:

Size		
12	10 m	(11 yd)
14	10 m	(11 yd)
16	10.20 m	($11\frac{1}{4}$ yd)
18	10.40 m	($11\frac{1}{2}$ yd)
20	10.50 m	($11\frac{2}{3}$ yd)

Fastening: 1 hook and bar, and 1 press stud

Strapless top

Cutting out

Strapless bodice (full-size pattern), lengthened to tuck in as described on page 33 for a drop waist:
2 × back, to fold
4 × side front
2 × CF, to fold
1 × 2.5 cm (1 in) bias strip × 1.40 m ($1\frac{2}{3}$ yd), for the boning

Sewing

1. Follow instructions 1–4 on page 73, omitting the first instruction to gather CF. Complete the top by following instructions 5–6 on page 74.
2. *Pleated frill.* Make and press the joins if necessary. Place the ribbon RS up on RS raw edges of the frill, allowing the ribbon to extend 2 mm ($\frac{1}{16}$ in). Stitch along the centre of the ribbon to attach.

Make pleats as follows, marking them with pins. The easiest way to do this is to pin a few pleats, secure them by stitching at the back of the frill, pin several more and stitch, and so on. Starting 4 cm ($1\frac{1}{2}$ in) from one end, mark with a pin every 5 cm (2 in). With the frill RS up and keeping the side edges level, bring the first pin to meet the third and stitch at the back, bring the fourth pin to meet the sixth and stitch, and so on in this sequence to the end. Flatten each pleat so the second, fifth and eighth pins touch the anchor stitch; machine along the middle of the frill to hold the box pleats in position, using a large machine stitch.

Apply the frill to RS bodice. Fold under the raw ends and pin beside the hooks and eyes. Pin the frill at intervals along the centre to the edge of the bodice, so that the frill extends. Pull up the machine stitching, using it as a gathering thread, until the frill lies flat on the bodice. Finish by stitching along the middle of the frill. The stitching should just miss the ends of the Rigilene boning, although the needle will not break if you do happen to sew through it.

Skirt

Cutting out

Straight skirt (full-size pattern), lengthened to the ankle as shown on page 37:
1 × back, to fold
1 × front, to fold

Allocate space for the waistband to be cut later. Mark the darts, front tucks and zip point.

Sewing

1. Follow instructions 1–9 on pages 80–81, omitting the lining.
2. *Centre back frill.* Place the ribbon RS up on RS long edges of the frill, allowing the ribbon to extend 2 mm ($\frac{1}{16}$ in). Stitch along the centre of the ribbon to attach. Make nine pleats as follows, Starting 7 cm ($2\frac{3}{4}$ in) from the wide end, mark with a pin every 12 cm ($4\frac{3}{4}$ in) in the centre of the frill. Fold, pin and stitch each fold in the same way as the bodice frill, finishing by stitching along the centre with a large stitch.

Pin the frill RS up on RS back skirt, matching the centre of the frill to CB. Leave the unfinished ends extending and pull up the gathering thread until the frill lies flat on the skirt. Turn under and stitch a hem across both ends of the frill so that the edges are level with the base of the waistband and the finished hem of the skirt. Complete the skirt by stitching along the centre of the frill.

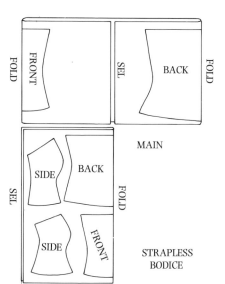

MAIN

SIDE BACK

SIDE FRONT

STRAPLESS BODICE

FOLD · FRONT · SEL · BACK · FOLD

SEL · FOLD

CONTRAST FRILLS

FRONT FRILL (BODICE)

BACK FRILL (SKIRT)

SEL · FOLD

5 Decoration

Esmé House was teaching at Yeovil College when I went to see what was a stunning exhibition of students' work. The work was both artistic and practical, and Esmé's enthusiasm and encouragement brought out talents the students didn't know they had.

One aspect that interested me was how, in several instances, one basic design was used repeatedly but with different techniques. The development of a piece of lovely decorative work from such a simple start led me to ask Esmé to produce a couple of outlines for this book, with some suggestions for treatment.

I am indebted to Esmé for her contribution to the following section.

Decorative Features

It is worth spending time on decorative features, for it is the addition of such things that makes your clothes individual and worthy of attention. The suggested outlines are followed by a selection of decorative features, with suggestions as to where they could be used. In addition you will, of course, have your own ideas.

Design 1

A star-shaped geometric design that can be outlined and worked using various techniques:

(a) Take the radials separately and re-arrange them. Three arrangements are illustrated. Not only does the shape change but so does the focal point, and this will govern how you decide to work the design.

Design 1

(b) Trace the hole in the middle of one shape and you have a different style of design. Cut it in half and overlap it as shown, and it looks like a row of squatting figures.

(c) The diamond shapes can be separated and spread, or cut in half and rejoined.

(d) Remove the centre from the original design and replace it with another shape.

(e) Use the centre on its own.

Variations on Design 1

112

Design 2

Overlapping circles are slightly more versatile. Follow their progress as the design is broken up:

(a) the centre and shaped sections

(b) using only the centre

(c) a border using the shapes

    With both designs, the choice of colour and texture will create even more variation.

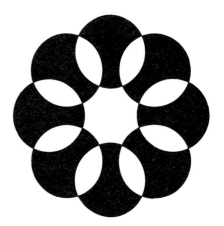

Design 2

Decorative Techniques

Mark out the shape of the garment or article, but do not cut it out. Leave plenty of surplus fabric all round the edge. Make sure your design will fall within the garment seam allowances.

    Mark the design out on the fabric with small basting stitches and silk thread, or No. 50 Anchor Machine Embroidery thread, so that the stitches can be removed later without damage to the fabric. There should be no need to mark all the details of the design, simply the guidelines.

Random stitching

This is easy to do and suitable for small areas such as a bag or bodice panel. The stitching can be worked from RS or WS; your choice will depend on the thread you use. Matching or contrast sewing thread such as Drima may be used on top and underneath, and you stitch from RS. Fine gold and silver thread can be used on top with sewing thread underneath, in which case stitch from RS but loosen the top tension. Heavier, contrast or gold or silver thread must be wound onto the bobbin so you then stitch from WS, loosening the bottom tension a little.

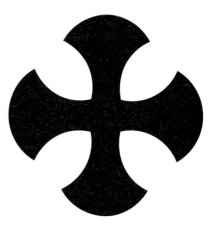

1. Stretch the fabric taut in an embroidery hoop. Remove the machine foot and drop the feed teeth. (Refer to the machine manual for instructions.)

2. Remember to lower the lever, even though there is no sewing foot. Practise before starting on the garment.

3. Work the stitching, manoeuvring the frame until the entire panel is covered.

4. Remember to raise the teeth, attach the foot and restore the tension afterwards.

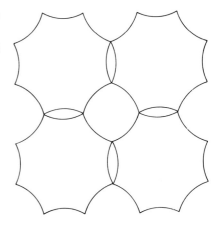

Variations on Design 2

113

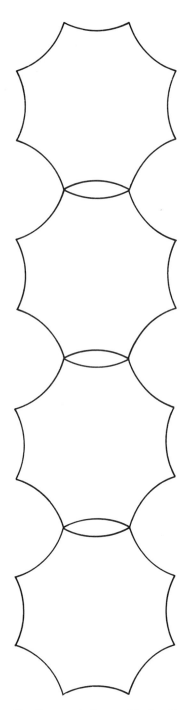

Further variation on Design 2

Appliqué

Appliqué is a very versatile decoration, suitable for any area of dress, jacket or bag, using matching or contrast fabric.

1. Press Bondaweb to the back of the appliqué fabric.
2. Select your motif, and outline the number you require on the fabric.
3. Cut out the motifs and arrange them on the base fabric. When you have decided on suitable positions, peel off the paper backing and press the motifs in place. Stitch around each one using satin stitch. Add beads, pearls, sequins, rosettes and embroidery as appropriate.

Shadow appliqué

This kind of appliqué can be worked on a jacket made from fine or transparent fabric. Use either the same fabric or one that contrasts effectively when placed underneath. The contrast can be slightly stiffer than the main fabric. The thread can match the main fabric, or it can be gold or silver. Work the appliqué as late as possible to get the position correct.

1. Cut a piece of appliqué fabric, put it beneath the main fabric and baste.
2. Select motifs and decide with the use of paper templates where they should be placed. Outline the motifs on the appliqué fabric.
3. Stitch along the outlines, through both layers. This may be done by hand using herringbone stitch worked right across the motif, or by machine using a small straight stitch.
4. Alternatively the design can be marked on the upper fabric and outlined with back stitch, or by machine, using a narrow space twin needle.
5. On the underside, carefully cut away the contrast fabric around each motif, trimming close to the stitching. A variation is to cut away the fabric within each motif.

Complete the garment and add any additional decoration.

Crushed appliqué

This decoration uses scraps of soft fabric that match or contrast with the main fabric. The fabric is squashed into an irregular shape. The shapes can be used separately, but they look more effective if several are nestled together on a bag or bodice, or even around a hemline. Work the decoration as late as possible in the construction.

1. Cut circles of fabric. In fact, irregular shapes can also be used so there is no need to cut accurately. The size of the pieces depends on the proportion of the design required.
2. Fold under a 3 mm ($\frac{1}{8}$ in) single hem onto WS and insert a gathering thread through the edge.
3. Pull up the gathers fairly tightly and fasten off the thread.
4. Attach the shapes to the base fabric. This is best done if the base fabric can be inserted in an embroidery frame. Mark out the area

of the design on RS, using fabric pen or tailor's chalk. Stitch from WS base fabric, first placing the shape in position on RS. Pass the needle through the base, through the centre of the gathered edge and out through the opposite side of the puff. Stab the needle down again through shape and base. Continue in this way, stabbing at random through the shape to leave a bubbled effect. Make sure the outer edge of the shape covers the gathered edge. Beads and pearls can be added afterwards or applied with the stab stitching. Do not press.

Quick appliqué

As its name suggests, this is very simple to do. Lace motifs, for example, can be used to decorate a jacket or dress. It is particularly effective on transparent fabric such as chiffon.

1. Select suitable small areas of lace and cut out, allowing 3 mm ($\frac{1}{8}$ in) all round.
2. Press Bondaweb to WS motifs, laying them on greaseproof paper first so that the Bondaweb does not penetrate to the ironing board cover. Use a warm iron and damp muslin cloth, and make sure the Bondaweb sticks firmly in place.
3. Decide on positions for the motifs. Peel off the paper backing, trim off the surplus 3 mm ($\frac{1}{8}$ in) all round, place each motif in position on RS garment and press. Once again, use a warm iron and damp cloth.

Add beads or pearls if appropriate.

Motif quilting

1. Prepare three layers of fabric: garment fabric, wadding and backing fabric. This is usually muslin but could be lining, in which case the garment would be finished with binding round the outer edge. Cut all the pieces much bigger than the pattern piece to be cut out later.
2. Place the backing material on a table WS up, with the wadding on top and the fabric RS up on top of that. Carefully baste all together. Begin at the centre and baste out to the sides, dividing the area into four. Constantly smooth out the fabric in front of the needle. Baste all over the piece, vertically and horizontally, with rows placed about 3–4 cm ($1\frac{1}{4}$–$1\frac{1}{2}$ in) apart.
3. Make paper copies of your chosen motif and use it to make the design, arranging all the motifs on the fabric. Do this in conjunction with the garment pattern. Mark the position of each motif with small basting stitches or fabric pen, beside the edge of the paper. Alternatively attach the paper to the fabric with a few stitches and use the edge of the paper as a guide when stitching.
4. Using matching or contrast thread and medium-length straight stitch, machine around the motif. Turn the corners carefully, with the needle down in the fabric. If you are working a geometric motif, count the stitches for accuracy.
5. On WS, pull both machine thread ends through, thread into a needle and work a few stitches through the backing to fasten off.

6. Place the garment pattern on the quilting and cut out. Make up and finish before removing the quilting lines.

Ribbon embroidery

This uses 3 mm ($\frac{1}{8}$ in) wide satin ribbon to create areas of texture.
1. Apply soft iron-on Vilene to WS fabric.
2. Mark out a design on the fabric using fabric pen.
3. Starting at a raw edge or at a point on the design where the ribbon ends can be concealed, stitch the ribbon to the fabric, following the outline. Use a small straight stitch. Do not press.

Ribbon weaving

This attractive decoration is ideal for small, flat areas such as a bag or bodice panel. Work the weaving before cutting the area to size. Use single satin ribbon or two or three different types of ribbon together, such as velvet, jacquard and satin. The ribbon can be one colour or mixed colours can be used.
1. Assemble the panel on the ironing board. Cut a piece of soft iron-on Vilene 5 cm (2 in) bigger all round than the area to be covered.
2. Cut a few lengths of ribbon longer than required and arrange in a plain or twill weave sequence, threading them over and under to obtain a pattern. Pleasant optical illusions are possible.
3. Having worked out a sequence, arrange the ribbons on the Vilene. Press carefully all over to attach the ribbon to the Vilene.
4. Put the panel pattern on the weaving and stitch round the outer edge. Cut out just outside the stitching. When you make up the garment, back this area with fabric or lining.

Ribbon point edging

An attractive edging for the flap of a bag, the upper edge of the camisole or strapless bodice, the edge of the jacket or the neckline of the cap-sleeved top. Made in wide ribbon, it also looks good along each edge of a skirt hemline slit, even along the hemline itself.

It is easier to make neat, even points if the garment edge is completed first. For one thing it is easier to centre the points and balance the design, but also the ribbon tends to become crushed if sandwiched between layers of fabric and stitched. If you cannot avoid having a lining or facing on top, sew it in place by hand.

Use single satin polyester ribbon of any width over about 13 mm ($\frac{1}{2}$ in).
1. Starting at the right and with the garment edge WS towards you, fold the ribbon over to make a point. Place it against the edge with the horizontal edge close to the garment edge.
2. Make a few back stitches to hold the ribbon edges together just below the garment edge, also taking the thread through the fabric, although not through to RS.
3. Fold the ribbon so that it turns through 180 degrees and extends beyond the garment edge. Take a couple of stitches

through the ribbon edges. Fold the ribbon again and stitch.
4. Proceed in this way until the edging is complete. Either side of the points can be RS; both sides are equally attractive. Do not press.

Ribbon carnations

These are simple to make and look effective used singly, in a row attached to a shoulder strap or dress edge, or in clusters on a bag or on clothes.
1. Use double satin polyester ribbon; the wider the width, the bigger the flowers. For ribbon 13 mm ($\frac{1}{2}$ in) wide, cut pieces 18 cm (7 in) long and join the ends to make a circle.
2. Using thread to match perfectly, start with a knot and insert a gathering thread along one edge. Pull up the thread tightly, secure with a couple of stitches then take the needle through the shoulder strap or garment fabric.
3. The centres can be filled with clusters of beads or French knots. Alternatively, use 3 mm ($\frac{1}{8}$ in) satin ribbon, possibly in a contrast colour, and make four or five loops in the middle of each flower. Thread the ribbon into the eye of a large needle and use it to make the loops, stabbing back and forth and taking the ribbon under the base fabric between flowers.
4. If wide ribbon is used for the flowers, an inner line of petals can be made, using a narrower ribbon, before filling the centres. Do not press.

Zigzag ribbon

This makes useful textured solid decoration to use as centres; it also looks very attractive in straight lines.

Use single or double satin polyester ribbon, or gold or silver ribbon and thread to match the colour.
1. Cut a length of ribbon, fold under 6 mm ($\frac{1}{4}$ in) at each end then insert a gathering thread, starting with a knot. Use the knot to hold one end under and work running stitch in an even zigzag pattern.
2. When you reach the end, pull up the thread tightly and form the ribbon into a circle, joining the two folded ends with oversewing.
3. Flatten the motif and attach it to the background fabric. The centre can be filled with beads, French knots or tiny loops of narrow ribbon. Alternatively place flat on finished edge of garment and stitch in place.

It is not possible to give widths of ribbon or amounts to gather, nor how to space the gathering. It is best to experiment once you have selected your ribbon. Do not press.

Ribbon points

Overlapping folds of ribbon can be arranged in lines, stars, circles or fan shapes. Interesting shaded effects can be created by using various colours. Use double satin polyester ribbon so that the design does not flatten or become crushed.

1. Attach soft sew-in or iron-on Vilene to WS fabric. Mark out the area of the garment pattern but do not cut out. Mark a few guidelines for the ribbon design, using fabric pen, basting or embroidery pencil. There is no need to transfer all the detail. If possible, put the fabric into an embroidery frame.

2. Any width of ribbon can be used, depending on how bold the finished design is to be. The width of ribbon governs the size of the point, and this in turn governs the length of each point. Experiment with the ribbon before deciding on the length. The design shown in the photograph was made using 10 mm ($\frac{3}{8}$ in) satin ribbon cut in 6 cm ($2\frac{1}{2}$ in) lengths.

3. Work out which way you want the points to overlap and begin with the one that will be underneath. Remember that the final join will have raw edges to be covered with beads, gathered ribbon, etc.

4. Using a small needle and thread to match the ribbon, fold the first piece in half and overlap the ends. Attach it to the fabric with one oversewing stitch at the point, take the needle to WS and bring up at the base, work three straight overcast stitches across the base and take the needle to WS. Fold the next piece of ribbon, place in position to overlap the first point by about one-third, bring the needle up and sew through the point, then secure the base of the point. Continue in this way until the design is complete.

5. Remove the frame, check the size and position of the pattern outline, and cut out. Do not press.

Ribbon roses

Easy to make, these fabric roses are very effective and eye-catching. Use them singly or make a spray for a bag, hat, neckline or waist. Use single satin ribbon 1 cm ($\frac{3}{8}$ in) or more in width; the wider the ribbon, the bigger the rose. You will need thread to match, and also florist's wire and green tape.

1. Cut a length of wire 10 cm (4 in) long, which can be trimmed later if necessary. Bend over 1 cm ($\frac{3}{8}$ in) at one end. Slip one end of the ribbon under the wire hook and wind the ribbon round several times. Anchor with a couple of stitches at the base of the ribbon.

2. Fold the ribbon across at right angles, satin side uppermost, and again use the thread to hold it at the edge. Wrap the ribbon round several times, holding it tightly against the wire at the base; insert a few stitches to secure. This forms the tight centre of the rose.

3. Fold the ribbon over at right angles again, and wind it round the wire.

4. Continue in this way, folding and winding and bringing the base of the rose further down the wire to fan out the top. The bloom can be made as tight or as full as you wish.

5. Wrap green tape round the base and down the wire to finish.

Join several roses together, adding leaves if you wish. Ribbon loops can also be attached. Colour can be introduced in the middle of the rose.

Buds can be made by using narrow ribbon and omitting the wire.

Ribbon rosettes

Use single satin ribbon 5 mm ($\frac{1}{4}$ in) long and matching thread.

1. Gather the ribbon along one edge and pull up the gathers tightly. From this calculate whether you need a longer or shorter length, depending on the width of the ribbon, and cut pieces to make the number of rosettes required.

2. Fold under one end of the ribbon, gather all the pieces and pull up. Thread a needle with the gathering thread and sew through the centre to secure.

3. Make sure the raw edge of the ribbon is not obvious. Apply a drop of Fray Check to the end of the ribbon.

4. Sew a bead, drop pearl or ball button to the centre. Alternatively, make a tiny rosette from narrow lace edging and sew to the centre. Lace edging wider than the ribbon can also be added to the rosette, placing it under the ribbon and gathering both together.

Flowers and feathers

Petals are easy to make from fabric, and feathers are very useful for representing leaves or more petals. The assembled flowers can be used on a hat, bag, shoulder strap, strapless dress, belt or as a corsage on a coat or jacket.

You will need fabric such as satin or taffeta, thread to match, firm iron-on Vilene and some small beads or pearls.

1. To make a flower, draw one petal on cardboard and cut out. Divide the fabric in half and outline the template on RS of one half. Draw five petals for each flower, using fabric pen.

2. Press iron-on Vilene to WS of the remaining half of the fabric. Place both pieces of satin together, WS together, and baste. Stitch around all the petal outlines with a small, close zigzag stitch. Carefully trim around each petal, snipping away the fabric close to the stitching, then stitch around again.

3. Sew three rows of beads along each petal, spacing out those at the end of each row, then thread a number of varied beads onto the needle, attaching the end to the base of the petal. Line up five petals and insert a running stitch along the edges of them all. Pull up the thread so that the petals stand up. Lift each one and stitch it on the underside to the next petal, overlapping the edges.

4. Sew a large bead, pearl or drop bead in the centre of the flower. Arrange three feathers in half-circles and sew the flower to the middle.

Fabric flowers

You can make separate petals of varying sizes, to build up into flowers. Use crisp fabric; reinforce it with iron-on Vilene if necessary before cutting the petals.

1. Cut squares of fabric to the following sizes: one × 5 cm (2 in) for the bud centre, two × 6 cm ($2\frac{3}{8}$ in), three × 7 cm ($2\frac{3}{4}$ in), and four or five × 9 cm ($3\frac{1}{2}$ in).

2. Fold each square of fabric RS out, corner to corner.

3. Using a long double thread, gather along both straight edges through both layers and pull up the thread until the fabric curls into a petal shape, then fasten off.

4. Beginning with the bud centre, roll the smallest petal up after gathering, back stitch to hold the thread then fold and attach petals the next size up, and so on.

5. Stitch firmly through the bases to fasten off.

6. Place in position on the garment and back stitch from WS through to the flower, stitching in a circle and making sure all raw edges on RS are concealed.

For a full-blown rose, turn the petals back.

Rouleau swirls

These can be used as buttons on fine fabrics, or on the outside of a garment when another fastening such as hooks or Velcro has been used. Swirls look attractive clustered on a bag; sewn singly to the corners of a jacket collar; in a row at the fastening edge of a belt; or the pleated belt or spaced out around the waistline of a strapless dress.

1. Make a long piece of corded rouleau (see below).

2. Fold under the end to form the centre, then wind the rouleau round it several times until you have the size you want. For a single swirl, trim the end and tuck it underneath, holding the swirl together with a few stitches, then sew it to the garment. It you are making a row of swirls, continue to the next one and wind it in the opposite direction.

Rouleau flowers

Made in the same fabric as your outfit, one of these flowers is a novel decoration on a hat, bag, jacket or dress.

1. Cut strips of bias fabric 2 cm ($\frac{3}{4}$ in) wide. Join to make about 1 m (1 yd) length. Press to stretch, then fold RS together.

2. Stitch with a slight zigzag stitch; place the fold of the fabric to the right, and keep the stitching even by having the edge of the foot level with the fold. (In fine fabrics, the rouleau can be narrower; adjust the width by moving the needle position off centre.) Leave long ends of thread at one end.

3. To turn RS out, insert a rouleau needle and sew the eye to the corner of the rouleau, using the ends of thread. Ease the fabric onto the needle and pull through.

4. Hold up the length of rouleau, take one end and form a loop like a petal. With a needle and matching thread, sew through to hold. Make another loop at the back and stitch.

5. Continue like this, varying the size of the loops, until you have a pleasing shape and size. Cut off the surplus or leave trailing ends, and stitch the flower to the garment. Alternatively, attach it to a brooch pin or hair grip.

Cover the centre with a bead, pearl, small button, lace rosette or stick-on diamanté trimming.

Cutwork

In this technique, the fabric is cut away after stitching. It can be used for single motifs or a border.
1. Outline the design on Stitch 'n' Tear embroidery paper, on a piece long enough to cover the area to be decorated.
2. Baste the Stitch 'n' Tear to WS main fabric.
3. Stitch round the outline with satin stitch and ease away the Stitch 'n' Tear. Carefully trim away surplus fabric.

Pintucks

Work the tucks before cutting the fabric as there is no accurate way of calculating how much fabric the tucks will use.
1. Beginning at the centre, fold and press a crease. Edge stitch the tuck and press.
2. Using an adjustable marker, measure, press and stitch a second tuck. Continue in this way until you have an area from which you can cut a pattern piece.

Corded pintucks

Fabric that has been tucked horizontally in this way makes an attractive hem band. A pretty ruched effect can be produced by pulling up the cord in parallel tucks.
   Use a twin needle, two reels of matching thread and a large size straight stitch and thin crochet cotton.
1. Mark the fabric with lines on RS.
2. Feed the end of the crochet cotton up through the hole in the machine plate in front of the needle hole. Pull the cotton under the foot towards the back; have the rest running free on the floor.
3. Stitch on the marked lines then continue making parallel tucks, using the foot to space them evenly, until you have the design you want.

Trapunto

This technique could be described as padded tucks. It is particularly effective when worked as three or four lines outlining the edge of a garment. It is suitable for all fabrics except those that are extremely transparent.
1. Select a design and outline it on muslin or a similar soft, open fabric such as voile. Baste this to WS fabric.
2. Stitch round the outline with hand running stitch or a straight machine stitch.
3. Make a second line of stitching outside the first and parallel to it. The distance between the rows depends on the thickness of yarn used for padding.
4. On WS, use a bodkin to thread a strand of thick wool between the stitching, making a hole in the muslin where the ends will protrude.

Shell edgings

The technique makes a pretty finish on the edges of frills. It is not suitable for thick fabrics.

Hand shell hem

1. Trim the fabric edge, leaving a 5 mm ($\frac{1}{4}$ in) seam allowance. Fold a small double hem onto WS, baste and press.
2. Stitch the hem by sliding the needle through the hem fold for 5 mm ($\frac{1}{4}$ in) or so then take the needle right over the hem twice, pulling the thread to wrinkle the fabric slightly.
3. Remove the basting very carefully. Press lightly.

Machine shell hem

1. Attach the shell hem foot to machine, and set to zigzag or blind hem stitch.
2. Trim the fabric edge cleanly to leave slightly more than 5 mm ($\frac{1}{4}$ in) for the hem and feed it through the foot. (Try this technique on spare fabric as there is a knack of holding the edge of the fabric upright as it goes through the foot.)

Suffolk puffs

These make an attractive crunchy decoration using small pieces of fabric that match or contrast with the background. They can be clustered together or used singly on a bag, or even applied all over a strapless bodice. Use fairly soft but springy fabric so that the puffs retain their shape.

1. Cut pieces of fabric, one for each puff. The finished puff will be half the size of the circle, so you may need to experiment to find the size you want. Press the circles.
2. Fold under a 3 mm ($\frac{1}{8}$ in) single hem onto WS and insert a gathering thread through the edge. Alternatively zigzag over the raw edge and insert a gathering thread just inside the stitching.
3. Pull up the gathering thread tightly and sew in the thread end securely. Flatten the puff a little.
4. Arrange the puffs as required and stitch to base fabric using stab stitches concealed inside, or back stitch worked from WS base fabric.

The decorations on the bag on page 85 are sewn very securely to withstand the obvious wear; those on the dress are connected by a thin plait of thread.

Beads and pearls can be added to the design. Do not press.

6 *Finishing Touches*

Loops and hangers
Some garments are difficult to hang up, some slip off the hanger in the wardrobe. Use lengths of ribbon or make tubing from spare pieces of fabric. The tubing can be on the bias or SG. The length of the loop depends on where it is attached.

On strapless dresses, make loops 10–12 cm (4–4½ in) long, double and sew to the waist join near the seams. Hang the dress inside out with the bodice inside the skirt. For trousers, make loops 7 cm (3 in) long, double and sew under the edge of the elastic casing, at CB and CF or at each side. Loops for skirts can be the same length and sewn to the side seams at the base of the waistband. For the cap-sleeve and camisole garments, make very long loops and attach to the side seams below the armholes. Adjust the length so that the loops pass over the hook of the coathanger.

Shoulder strap retainers
These may be needed for cap-sleeve garments with a low neck. Although they are available in the shops, it adds a finishing touch if you make your own. Use ribbon 6 mm (¼ in) wide, allowing about 8 cm (3½ in) for each. Fold a 1 cm (⅜ in) double hem at each end of the ribbon and hem round. Sew a tiny press stud to the ends. Open the press stud and place the ribbon along the shoulder seam about 4 cm (1½ in) from the neck edge. Back stitch in place.

Lining
Instructions for lining are included only where the garment in the photograph was lined. Any of the clothes, including trousers, can be lined if you wish. Use the same pattern pieces as for the garment, but shorten them a little to make the lining 1–3 cm (⅜–1¼ in) shorter at the hemline.

Make up the lining, including any adjustments made to the garment. Leave the zip opening at the right seam instead of the left. Save time and thread by neatening the raw edges of seams from hem to thigh level only. Turn up and stitch the lining hem with a straight or decorative stitch, or add a lace edging. Press the lining.

Put the lining inside the garment, lifting it so that the hem is at the correct level, and pin it to the garment along the waist, upper edge, neckline, etc. If the lining is slightly loose, so much the better; if there is a strain on the lining, it will not wear very well. Ease in any fullness. Back stitch the lining to the seam allowance of the garment then complete the garment with a waistband, binding, elastic or whatever is called for.

Finish by making a bar tack between the garment and the lining on each side seam about 10–14 cm (4–5$\frac{1}{2}$ in) above the hem. Work four strands of thread 2 cm ($\frac{3}{4}$ in) long between the seam allowances and cover them with loop stitch, worked close together.

Continuous bias

When you need long pieces of bias fabric, cut it in one long strip, as follows. Cut a large rectangle of fabric and mark bias lines the width required at an angle of 45 degrees on WS fabric, using tailor's chalk or fabric pen. Cut off the unmarked opposite corners. Fold the fabric RS together, place the cut edges together but so that the width of one strip is left extending. Stitch the join and press open. Cut the strip, cutting round the tube.

Buttons and loops

The patterns in the book are easy to make partly because I have kept fastenings to a minimum. However, there are several places where you might like to attach a ball button and rouleau loop.

The jacket could be fastened edge to edge at the base of the flounce collar with a single loop and button. The shaped belt and wide pleated belt could be fastened with several placed close together. If you are making the cap-sleeved pattern with a round neck back and front, the neckline will have to be made bigger to get it over your head. This may be done by cutting it lower; the alternative is to leave one shoulder seam open for 2.5 cm (1 in), press the seam so that the edges meet, and attach a button and loop after completing the neck finish.

Use a length of rouleau with piping cord inside for both buttons and loops. Calculate approximately what length will be required, and allow twice the amount of thin piping cord. Calculate the width of fabric by wrapping it round the cord and adding a 2 cm ($\frac{3}{4}$ in) seam allowance. Cut a length of bias fabric to the width measurement. Wrap the fabric round the cord, WS out, starting in the centre of the length of cord. Attach a zip foot or piping foot to the machine and stitch across the cord to secure the end of the fabric, then turn and sew to the end alongside the piping. Trim the seam allowance and turn the rouleau RS out by pulling the short end of the cord and pushing the fabric back over the other end. Trim off the surplus cord.

To make a ball button, make a double loop and thread the end in and out of the loops. Pull the ends gently to form a button. Trim the ends and stitch together. Sew onto the surface of the fabric, or make a hole in the fabric with a bodkin and pass the ends through. Secure strongly on the inside of the garment.

To make a loop, cut a length of rouleau and oversew the ends together, leaving a hole big enough to go over the button. Attach to the garment as for the button. If the loops are going to be on RS garment, use a longer length and sew into a frog shape, allowing one loop to pass over the button.

Waistline stay

Fitted dresses, particularly those without straps, are easier to wear if a stay is attached to the inside waistline. This includes drop-waist designs.

Use grosgrain ribbon 1–2 cm ($\frac{3}{8}$–$\frac{3}{4}$ in) wide or, for a tighter fit, used curved petersham. Measure the grosgrain round your waist, not too tightly, add 4 cm ($1\frac{1}{2}$ in) and cut. Fold back and stitch the ends and attach a hook and eye to fasten the stay end to end. It should fit your waist comfortably when fastened.

Fold in four and mark the quarters with fabric pen. Have the dress WS out, with the zip fastened. Place the stay, with the hook fastened, so that one edge is on the dress seam allowance and the grosgrain extends towards the skirt. Pin the stay to the dress at the quarters. In the case of drop-waist dresses, there will be no waist join to follow so pin it to the lining. You may need to put the dress on to check the position.

Attach the stay to the dress with a bar tack on each side of the zip, between the stay and the side seam allowance. For the remainder, either hem all round along one edge of the grosgrain or make several more bar tacks at the seams, CF, CB, etc. The latter finish is best for the looser-fitting ruched or drop-waist bodice as it will allow the dress to keep its shape while the stay remains in place.

Safety ties

If you do not insert a stay as described above, take the following precaution to make sure that the zip is not strained. Cut two pieces of tape or narrow ribbon 30 cm (12 in) long and sew them to the waist seam inside the dress, stitching one each side of the zip. The tapes are tied to draw the zip edges close together when the zip is fastened.

Fabric Stockists

TURQUOISE SILK (PAGE 72)
Far East Fabrics
Dartington Hall
Tavistock
Devon PL19 8DH
Tel (0822) 4501
Mail order. Range of Thai silks;
lots of colours, some stripes.

SEA GREEN AND LAKE GREEN
WILD SILK (PAGE 85)
Sussex Silks
Oakenwood House
Cinder Hill
Horsted Keynes
Haywards Heath
West Sussex
Tel (04447) 3630
Mail order. A range of more
than 40 delightful colours,
including some striped and
shot fabrics.

GOLD TISSUE FABRIC (PAGE 83);
PURPLE PAILLETTES JERSEY AND
PURPLE POLYESTER CRÊPE
(PAGE 87)
Alexander Fabrics
131 High Street
Epsom
Surrey
Tel (03727) 27724
Wide range of fabrics,
including theatrical.

BLACK POLYESTER SATIN AND
RED, CREAM AND BLACK PRINTED
POLYESTER (PAGE 91); BLUE AND
BLACK SATIN-STRIPED POLYESTER
VOILE AND BLUE SHOT CHIFFON
(PAGE 99)
Singer Shop
Altrincham
Cheshire
Extensive range of interesting
fabrics at reasonable prices.

BLACK AND WHITE SILK
JACQUARD (PAGE 75); JADE
GREEN SILK JACQUARD (PAGE 79)
Jacob Gordon Ltd
75 Duke Street
London W1
Tel (01) 629 5947
Luxurious couture fabrics from
the Continent.

RED AND BLACK PURE IRISH
LINEN (PAGE 86)
Craftswoman Fabrics
Unit 28
Kilroot Park Industrial Estate
Carrickfergus
Co. Antrim
Northern Ireland BT38 7DD
Tel (09603) 69277
Mail order (two catalogues
each year). Collections of
samples (small charge) divided
into natural fibre fabrics and
'out of this world' fabrics.
Excellent service and
tremendous variety of fabric.

MOIRÉ TAFFETA (PAGES 96 AND
98)
Silkworm
104 Warwick Street
Leamington Spa
Warwickshire CV32 4QP
Tel (0926) 313536
Comprehensive range of
evening and lingerie fabrics.
Silk specialists. Regular fashion
shows.

SILVER FABRIC (PAGE 104);
BRIGHT BLUE SPOTTED NET (PAGE
108)
Fabrics Galore
5 Church Street
Storrington
West Sussex
Tel (09066) 2074
Small but busy shop stacked
with a wide range of fabrics.
Very comprehensive
haberdashery. Regular fashion
shows.

PINK AND CREAM STRIPED SLUB
SILK (PAGE 77)
Silk Shades
33 Prentice Street
Lavenham
Suffolk CO10 9RD
Tel (0787) 247029
Specialists in silk and lace for
brides. Lovely selection. By
appointment only.

BLACK AND GOLD LACE (PAGE 94)
Rose and Hubble (various
stockists)

BLACK VELVET (PAGE 101)
Denholme Velvets (various
stockists)
A range of gorgeous colours.
Also wonderful embossed
velvets.

ACCESSORIES
Harlequin
Unit 25 Jubilee
Lawford
Manningtree
Essex CO11 1UR
Tel. 0206 396167
Mail order. Covered buttons
and belts as well as bags and
bows; also haberdashery.

Index

127